Pell-M

...So We Live!

Gilbert A. Sprauve, PhD

Order this book online at www.trafford.com
or email orders@trafford.com

Most Trafford titles are also available at major online book retailers.

Louis Ible, front cover art and layout.'
Singo Sprauve, photography for back cover.

Printed in the United States of America.

ISBN: 978-1-4269-5562-4 (sc)
ISBN: 978-1-4269-5563-1 (hc)

Library of Congress Control Number: 2011900669

Trafford rev. 03/17/2011

 www.trafford.com

North America & international
toll-free: 1 888 232 4444 (USA & Canada)
phone: 250 383 6864 ♦ fax: 812 355 4082

Pell-Mell (. . . So We Live!)

Gilbert A. Sprauve

THAT NESTING BUG

Skittish Parenting

"W'ere yo's own is?" The young man is addressing the nearest of two young ladies standing at the back of a vehicle in the parking lot of the mall. It's as if she has not heard him. So he repeats, just as the second woman moves off with her toddler in tow.

"W'ere yo's own is?"
"Ah ain' got none?"
"W-a-a-a? Yo' mean, you ain' got none?"
"S-o-o! Alyo' got to stop knockin' me up!"
"Yo got to gee' one!"
"An' you go support it?"

For the Want of an Aunt

A woman we know has this close friend who complained to her about the influence this woman's teen-age daughter has on a certain "brat." What did the girl do, and who is the "brat?"

"I don't want that brat calling me no *Auntie!*"

So then, what did the "brat" himself do? He *is*; that is the problem. That is the heart of the matter.

Our source and Sandy are friends, first of all, because Sandy is the former wife of this woman's brother-in-law. (Stay with us, kind Reader!) That brother-in-law was notoriously on the prowl long before he and Sandy divorced. In fact, he fathered a first child—while already having one at home— with a certain *other* woman.

The word "first" here alerts you, dear Reader, that it gets more complicated! When that child, only a toddler, got crushed under the shovel of a backhoe carrying out an excavation project in the neighborhood, Sandy let bygones be . . ., placed herself at the side of her rival and comforted her the night through, the way one cradles and pampers a listless, suffering child.

Our female informant, as close as she has become to her husband's ex sister-in-law—if one does indeed become an "ex" under the circumstances—couldn't tell you if the two women established a compact that gave Sandy to believe "it" would not happen again. When "it" did, Sandy, no less a Private Counsel and public figure than her spouse, called it "that."

This second child, born to "the other woman," by virtue of simply *being,* is the "brat."

Now, the home of our source's mother-in-law (and Sandy's former—if the term, etc., etc.), the mother of the men they married, (then!) is where a number of children are dropped off and picked up between school closing in the afternoon and dusk. When Sandy shows up for hers—who is a legitimate grand-daughter of the house, in Sandy's and our acquaintance's view, (anyway!)—the children flock to her and call her "Auntie." This is all right with her, except for the little boy whom she says her friend's almost sister-in-law's daughter encouraged to take that liberty! Hmmph!

Cyaant wait to father a daughter!

He saw the blue flashing lights of the patrol car through the glass door of the Mc Donald's as he was entering the fast food eatery.

Inside now, he could see, through the glass panels the two police squad cars sandwiching a late model off-white sedan in the drive-up lane. The atmosphere inside was thick with commentary on the event he had missed. The one contention that he could clearly decipher in the buzz behind and in front of the counter went something like this: "Did you see how that man hit the little girl? Boy, if it was my child…!"

He tried to tune in, but with so much to say by so many and with customers ordering their quarter-pounder or fish fillet, he gave up. In due time, one of the officers entered the establishment, picked up, from somewhere two pieces of black fabric and left. Evidently, crime scene evidence! A young woman with two teen-age girls asked to speak with the manager. He presented himself, and they went off in a corner and spoke. Afterward, she and the girls huddled by the door the cop had passed through.

Finally, the floor sweeper was close enough, and since he usually exchanges a pleasant greeting with him, he asked discreetly what the commotion was about. "Two Rasta had a argument. The one throw a punch at the other and the punch hit the child w'at was in the first one arms. Dat's w'en dey call de police!"

And while he was getting this relates from the orderly, a young man could be heard stating emphatically: "Punch de man li'l daughter like dat? 'Tain notting like dat go happen wid me! Punch my daughter like dat an' get away wid it? I cyaan' wait till I get my daughter, to see who go try dat!"

JUSTICE and NATURE; MAN MEETS BEAST

X-press Lane Justice

On this island a certain judge—a man with a solid social footing —held firmly to the rule: "first come, first served." In his court, whoever complained first could count on a favorable judgment. Mattie presented herself in his chambers one day with a complaint about verbal abuse from a former companion.

She had been "good" with this man till the day she decided to move out and take up residence with another man. According to Mattie, this was the day the slandering commenced. Her dismissed companion seemingly knew well her new goings and comings and would place himself along her path and loudly rant about female dogs. Mattie chose not to "take him on." Instead, she was presenting herself to the Court to register her complaint, namely about the barrage of invectives rained on her every time they crossed each other. The spurned companion was summoned and responded to the judge's probing by declaring:

"Judge, I never said a word to the woman!"
The judge then asked: "Did you make reference to a dog within ear shot of the woman?"
"Yes, but I never addressed her."
"Was there anyone else present?"
"No, your Honor."
"Did you see a dog in the area?"
"No, your Honor."
"Then, she wins the case; you're guilty!"

As the reader can imagine, this judge's way of finding for a complainant so summarily did not always sit well with the losing party.

The day would come when the guilty man would strike back at the magistrate with the rebuke: "So, you find me guilty, Judge, but just remember, as a lawyer, you never won a case!" "Say what you like! I'm winning this one, though!" he declared, as he slapped a heavy fine on the brash petitioner.

Escapade of the Blue Mongoose

In a way this story is a by-product of the Flash story in *Soundings over Cultural Shoals*. The person who related to me this story had been an early purchaser of Soundings and had made it a habit, when hailing me on the streets of St. John, to ask me which way my father's eccentric mount Flash went at the climax of her mad behavior. Finally, over drinks in Mooie's Bar one night, he explained how his query related to the Flash story.

It was in the days when the yard chicken—the one they now call "the free-roaming fowl"— was highly valued and in great demand, especially for the Sunday meal, but also for her eggs. Besides the high-soaring eagle-eyed chicken hawk, Mother Hen's greatest foe was the mongoose. If ever a small weasel-like creature possessed a bag of tricks that could always separate a fowl from her chicks, it was Brother Mongoose. And once he got the unschooled (usually first-time) mother and chicks separated, a tiny pip-squeak of a chicken was rapidly pounced on and devoured.

The clamor of the poultry farmer and, in turn, his clientele over these acts of larceny by the shifty rodent was great and, in these post-War years of lingering food scarcity, victory gardens and other authorized deeds of thrift and austerity, the authorities would not delay in setting a bounty on Brother Mongoose' hide! For each mongoose trapped and delivered to the Station, you were paid fifteen cents. (And fifteen cents meant something in those days!)

It was out of these circumstances that emerged the famous Cruz Bay Mongoose Races! This was a weekend affair. Which made sense, since the Bounty Paymaster wouldn't open again till Monday morning! So, what better way for the our young bucks to entertain themselves in this bayside town without enough flatland for a horserace or donkey race course, than to block off the straight and narrow main street that abutted the historic Lutheran Church, and pit the rust colored furry beasts against each other for wagers!

But then one had to be able to identify the runner in order to settle bets. This is when someone came up with the idea: Paint your mongoose the color

you choose! To the fainthearted who might protest,
the majority would argue: "His fate is sealed
anyway! What's the fuss about?" Not to mention the
bookish cynic (as in any group) who could cite his
research on scarifications, ridiculous frocking and
other disfigurements meted out to capital criminals
before rendering them lifeless!

So, on Mongoose Race Day, the fellows showed up,
this one with a red painted animal, the other with a
blue one, a green one, and so forth. The handlers
were adept at avoiding their sharp teeth. They
would be released from their cages with a string
attached either around the neck or to a leg, and
dash down the street. A winner would be declared,
and the animals would be retrieved for their
appointment with the Bounty Officer the following
day.

And so it went. Except, one Sunday when the blue
mongoose broke away from the paddock, made a
dash to the left and disappeared through the guinea
grass and wetland that ended, through sea grape
trees and heiters, at the water's edge. No one made
much of the evasion and escape.

But then, a few weeks later, a certain Mr. T., owner of a chicken farm a half-hour from town, in the adjoining bay, started noticing the regular disappearance of his baby chickens. He decided to keep watch for the thief, and indeed did catch the blue mongoose red-handed.

Well…caught in the act in the loose sense of the term! No one really dared lay hands on the blue mongoose. It was like he had earned his freedom in his own special way. Double jeopardy was not an option!

The Bear and the Lover of Gardens

In *Soundings* I told the story of a simple, unschooled workman who one day re-defined "communism" for me in words the oppressed immediately comprehend. On that occasion, S also set forth for me a critical rule for working with an uneducated and untrained labor force.

"I don't care how smart you are, Mister! If you are working with ten idiots, they will find a way to put their heads together and trip you up!"

Is it possible S had heard a version of the story related by La Fontaine in his Fables that went by the name "The Bear and the Lover of Gardens"?

A certain mountain Bear lived a solitary life in a distant forest. Loneliness was driving him mad. For, it is known that clear thinking and good sense soon abandon those who live alone!

(It is good to talk; [at times] it is better to remain silent! But both extremes are bad, says La Fontaine.)

No other animal ventured to where the Bear lived. So, he came to be horribly bored with his sad existence. While he was wallowing in his boredom, not far away, a certain Old Man was lamenting his similar lonely life. He was a lover of gardens and anything that bore flowers. However, while it makes good company, a garden does not speak!

So, tired of a life without conversation, one day the Old Man ventured into the woods to seek company. The bear, as things would have it, had descended from the mountain on a similar quest.

The two individuals ran into each other. The man was frightened, but what to do? The trick, he quickly realized, was to hide his fear and pretend to be unfazed. The Bear, without reserve, invited the Old Man to his place. The Old Man, instead, suggested they go to his house, promising a solid country meal of fruits from his garden, and milk. The Bear accepted, and before arriving, they were good friends.

Good friends they were, but for the whole day not a word was uttered by the Bear. Yet, better to be together in silence, than to be in the company of babbling fools, thought the Old Man. Besides, he could attend to his chores in peace.

The Bear went hunting for game and returned with it. His other principal task was that of Swatter of Flies—for bears engage almost incessantly in this activity! As the Old Man slept, he kept watch against troublesome flies. One day, while the Old Man was in a deep sleep, one of them landed squarely on his nose. The Bear could not believe the cheek of the little winged creature and set out to rid his old friend of the nuisance. Aware that his mighty paw might deal a mortal slap, he took hold of a rock, instead and threw it with such force that he crushed the fly…but also split the Old Man's head wide open. And, not better at reasoning than he was at throwing stones, he simply put the dead man to bed and called it that!

The advice that La Fontaine gives to us is: "There exists none more dangerous than an ignorant friend; better to have a wise foe!"

The Wolf and the Helpful Stork

The story is told by Jean de La Fontaine of how Brother Wolf one day was so reckless and impatient in devouring a meal of fresh meat that he soon found himself choking with a bone stuck in his lower throat. The pointed-beaked and long-necked stork, on one of her strolls, came upon the wolf who, by now, was rolling around on the ground and panting in distress. She asked what might be the problem.

Wolf muttered his predicament, and Stork offered to help: "Not to worry! With my long neck and beak…! Just open your mouth wide!"

In short order Stork had accomplished her task, had cleared the wolf's throat of the bone. And now she requested payment for her services.

"Payment! you said!" bellowed the Wolf. What cheek! You dare to ask for payment, after I was so good to let you place your head down into my throat and pull it back out without snapping it off with your disgusting long neck! This is a warning to never try that trick with me again!"

That is the day Sister Stork decided to keep her beak shut and only deliver babies—a service for which she has the good sense not to demand payment!

Wutless Work takes a break!

"Twenty-eight weeks looking for Work!" That's what the man being interviewed on NPR has just said to the interviewer. And the latter repeats, for effect. "Twenty-eight weeks looking for Work?"

Plunger seeks a commentary from the The Old Creole Sage, who seems always to be eavesdropping when such information reaches his ears.

"Lookin' fo' work all dis time, and he ain' got de good sense to stop lookin', since he ain' gon' fine it."

"An' why yo' say dat, Old Creole Sage?"

"Because, first of all, Work know he lookin' fo' it! Nex' t'ing, da was a white man complainin' 'bout couldn't fine work, right?"

"It could soun' so. Besides, if it was a black man, who would care?—wid all respect due to NPR!"

"Which goes straight to the point I am makin'!

Black man had his turn wid work. De man upstairs, a long time ago, sen' his message through de man at de pulpit an' wearin' de cloak: 'Just like Cleanliness is next to Godliness, no question asked, so you must work wid Work! Your rewards will be numberless. Trust me!'

"Trust? Did he say trust? De only reward Black man ever receive was countless deceptions an' beatings, till de day he decide he had enough! Dats de day he tell Work to go to Hell! An' furthermore, don' eva make de mistake to cross paths wid he again, or else…

"So now, wa happen since then is Black man and White man livin' more mix up wid each other— what dey call Integration. Work realize dat Black man ain' jokin', and as much as he would like to fraternize wid White man, he could only sneak aroun' at odd hours, like a werewolf stalkin' an' haunting a village. So, White man could only fantasize or have nightmares about meetin' up wid Work for de briefes' of moments.

"White man need to 'let it go,' like dey say," declares Ole Creole Sage. "Den he need to go back to de

Man Upstairs, and see if he got another plan!"

And, since we're talking about Work:

Here's the half of the conversation by cell phone that Plunger picked up as he waited to be served breakfast in Subway that Sunday morning: "Well...Dat ain' workin' fo' you? No! Don't do dat! Dat ain' no solution—holdin' two job! I tried dat, an' it didn't work fo' me! Yo' spen' all yo' time wid nottin' to do! It damn nearly kill me!"

LINGUAL
ENTICEMENTS

Bosom Lovers to this day!

It was Sunday just past noon when he came out the front door of the fast-food eatery and headed for his car. "Hello, Doc!"

He immediately recognized the melodious mature female voice, stopped and turned to see the still pretty oval face of the classy lady who had frolicked, in extremis, with him one night three decades ago—only a year or so into her widowhood.

He knew himself to be sweaty and raggedly-looking, having just had some stiff tennis exercises on this hot and humid day and wearing the now indispensable knee-support on the outside of his trousers, but dropped to the calf. She, on the other hand, judging by the time of the day and by her attire, which was becoming visible—and pleasantly and slightly teasingly so—as he approached the passenger front seat she occupied, was just coming from Church. Yet…, she uttered clearly the words: "Man, you're still in good shape!"

Then she proudly introduced the driver, who was
her grandson! "You know Doc?"

"I've heard of him," he said warmly, as they
exchanged handshakes through the lowered window
and across her still ample bosom. Then the young
man turned towards the drive-up window and
collected their order. As they drove off, he wished
them "A Happy Meal!"

De One fo' you an' de One fo' me

On the surface, it would appear far simpler to just utter the person's given name one time and be done with it. Be it Mina or Manny! However, the custom endures, particularly among our women here in the islands, at particular times, to refer to the Other as "De one fo' you" or "De one fo' Leona an' Raul!"

In our culture, it is tempting to tag such behavior as a manifestation of our humanizing—but, also, at times mischievous—penchant. So, you've at least given the individual in question—usually an offender, a miscreant, or "person of interest," anyway—some pedigree or parentage!

For me, it took a closer reading of an early childhood incident in Muriel Barbery's *L'Elégance du Hérisson* to better grasp the cultural nuances involved in this folk women's—for it is almost always they that do it—word play. The female narrator, in the story mentioned above, a Parisian concierge, tells of her personal epiphany the day way back in grade school when a teacher first called her by name! (At home, neither she nor her siblings had ever been addressed by name by their mother!)

Why would a woman—especially a mother—so harshly deny such convenient identity to her progeny, or, in our case, to any Tommy, Lucie or Teddy? Wouldn't it just be a major paradox of our own ethnolinguistic conduct here on these islands if it turned out that the very instincts that trigger the "He fo'" expressions are related to the ones that have come to block the casual "Who yo' fa?" query of the past? And that, while maternal curiosity and proprietary interest are operative in the second situation, the first is more linked to womanly solidarity in tracking and containing the errant male?

Far fetched? Yes! But let me explain! First, a bit of elementary Creole phonemics: The "fo'" and the "fa" mentioned above evidently have the same origins in the English word "for", particularly when it expresses possession or "destined for." The vowel has several allophones; when under stress in an utterance, however, it normally takes the form of "a" /huyofá/= Who you for = To whom do you belong?

Now, about "Who yo' fa?" In my growing up days on these islands the adult routinely posed this question to any unknown or unfamiliar youngster, especially if he or she presented him/herself in the company of one of your own household. This was done totally without malice or aforethought. All it was intended to produce was an identification of the child's parents or the person responsible for them.

There was absolutely no interest in establishing boundaries between insiders and outsiders! If any such thought entered the questioner's mind— through mischief—then he or she invariably added "but" and "at all." Hence: "But who yo fa, at all?" And that could be the prelude to the command: "Go 'mongst yo' sex!" Which, in turn, had nothing to do with "sex" as between consenting adults! It meant: "Go find your equals!"
But, back to "Who yo' fa?" and its late interdiction in our exchanges. The culprit, this writer suspects, is the overwhelming demographic pressures that have come to impact on the lives of our people on these islands. Our neighborhoods are now populated by cells of migrants from many places, not the least of which are those from our neighboring Caribbean

islands. While, on the surface and for the most part, we are one Caribbean people, with a common history of migrations to greener pastures and concomitant ghetto-ization wherever, with a high potential for empathizing with each other's errant lot, these cells have proven to be increasingly fertile fodder for political aspirants and other power brokers. Vigilantes we have, but to them falls the task of stoking the fires of dissension between the so-called "native" and migrant populations. "Who yo' fa?" is now perceived, often erroneously, as the principal spark that draws the line between who belongs and who doesn't. (Interestingly enough, in our sister islands of the BVI, in order to protect the rights of their out-migrants and secure some demographic and political stability for their locals, legislators there have created the legal status "belongers" for those living elsewhere who can claim a parent of local birth.)

Having been confronted by an adolescent with the question, "Why do you feel that we are different?" this writer, retired educator and community activist can easily concoct the situation at home wherein the elder questions then counsels the youngster, "Why did he ask you that? Go back tomorrow and ask him why he asked you that!" It is that kind of scenario that explains the demise of "Who yo' fa?" in our everyday talk in our island home. Now, as for "He fo' you" etc....This observer once approached a properly decked out man, homeward bound from a burial and its lavish reception; he inquired concerning the identity of the deceased. "Some good-fo'-nott'n; I don't even remember he name!" was the reply.

This folk moniker, "He fo' X," on the other hand, to the extent that 1) it fits into "woman talk" and 2) that our women bond with each other and share news and intelligence on topics of mutual benefit— however bizarre this benefit might seem to the outsider—is far from extinction through social interdiction of any kind anytime soon. This, for the simple reason that the expression lends itself well to codified well embedded behavior and information sharing, what some might call camaraderie gossiping. The following illustration needs little elaboration: Down on the beach by our fishing boats one day the guys were chatting about close encounters they had with their spouse over some adventure with another woman. As this kind of bragging goes, the closeness of the encounter, from one story to the other, intensified to the point where one fellow related the following:

He'd no sooner returned home from a cozy session with a sweetheart down the street, freshened up discretely and thrown himself down for a needed nap, when he thought he heard a familiar female voice excitedly trying to whisper the hottest piece of gossip to his spouse. It went something like this: "Yo' sure he fo' you sleepin? Wid my own two eyes I see de good-fo'-nottin' sneakin' in an' den out of she fo' de big guts policeman house dis afternoon!"

And who was the news carrier? A very recent rival of his spouse! After this tête-à-tête, these two women became the best of friends, "peas in a pod," the braggart reported, dusting his hands like a man done with a task or like one smacking his lips after a delicious meal. "Church out!" None of the fellows could beat that one!

Car control patrol

Elections are around the corner. It's the season for "gripin'-n-snipin'"! In a certain fast food eatery a male customer has seized the attention of the security guard, probably family or a close friend. He is ranting about this woman who is the daughter of his lady friend. In the guard he's found a sympathetic ear, though he is not a completely passive listener; he mutters an occasional comment on the protracted lamentation; short phrases like: "You're partly at fault! I wouldn't have done that." And so on.

Is the victimized really listening? His rant is non-stop: The woman moved in on her mother, claims to be giving care. Instead, she's grabbing everything she can get from her and living on her income. She has these children. She's not working!

"Then, the other day she tells me: her car needs a starting motor! What concern is that of mine? I ain' drive her. car! I ain' drive *in* her car!"

G.A. Sprauve

ODE TO
THE UNSUNG
DEPARTED

Pained Cranes Dozing

On a certain island in this chain now undergoing the onslaught of intense Development the following account was told to this writer, relative to the unexpected demise of a popular crane operator:

The man's body had been discovered in the sea one morning. Our informant reacted with the question: "M, who?" when he first heard the news. After which, he told his source that he hadn't even heard that the popular operator was missing; he was aware that he'd been "acting out" recently, essentially lamenting how the bigger picture was developing here on the islands. "Who was really in charge?" He was not necessarily listening to any input you might offer. But that was it!

Following the listener's reaction of shock, the news source rolled off the detail that the body had floated up, next to the public ferry dock after "People was asking each other, 'Who see M since two days ago, and where?'"

Our own source took the news back to his brother's

bedside, (the latter being in recovery from a partially paralyzing stroke he'd suffered almost two years ago) only to discover that he, a trade friend of M from their youth, too knew of the death but wasn't particularly surprised at the news. And no one was suggesting that foul play had anything to do with it.

Over the next few days, from various sources around their little seaport town, information became available that aided in assimilating his brother's lack of shock at a friend's tragic passing and that, furthermore, inclined our source to see a disturbing parallel between his brother's crisis of two years ago and M's inglorious exit from this life. Generational and Transitional issues, an expert might say!

"De man was drinkin' hard fo' 'bout two weeks! He left dis very bar—de laas night that anyone see him alive—pissed because I refused to sell him one more, went up de street lookin' fo' who would sell him more. Somebody say, dey see him up dere by de odda bar, flat on de groun', blockin' a man from movin' he jeep outta a parkin' space. Somebody went an' find one o' he closes' relative to get him on he feet an' get him down to de ferry dock.

"Some people believe he get on a ferry dat was docked there, to wait till the firs' trip in de mornin' to get back home. But den, somebody else ask: 'Which home? 'Tis a car de man livin' in fo' weeks!' De lang an' short of it: Some say, dey believe, de man wake up durin' de night, try to find heself, get disoriented an' walk overboard, an', not being a swimmer... Somebody else say, somebody see him in one o' de dinghies that duz tie up to de dinghy dock, dat tryin' to step off from it onto de dock... Then, there's the judgment call: "If de man close kin (or whoever it was) could accompany him to de ferry, to wait fo' tomorrow ferry, why he couldn' bring him to he own house to spend de night dere?" People are like that! They always know what somebody should have done for somebody else while they see nothing, hear nothing, do nothing!

Plunger has this cousin who is a natural born skeptic. When he related the tale of M's passing to the cousin, along with his speculation that depression was to blame for what eventually happened, the cousin, who had more than a passing acquaintance with M, raised an eyebrow and commented: "M??? With that empire the man built

for him and family, erecting buildings, raising
sunken boats, planting trees and poles? Hmm!"

Sure, the man had eventually acquired a fortune
with his crane, but who would recall that much of
his success had to do with his industry and
creativity? Which would leverage better deals for the
same cohorts who turned a cold shoulder when
help was so critically essential!

The story is told of how the bosses on one well
known Development project, hedging on paying
local operators the increased wages they were
demanding, decided to import drivers from the
neighboring island, while slandering the locals as
being less trained for the excavating projects on
hand. The company paid bonuses according to the
operator's skills demonstrated in adverse wind
conditions, when the competition normally
suspended operations.

M ran circles around the imported crane men!
How? From his apprenticeship with an exceptional
boat captain during his youth, he had learned and
guarded secrets on the whims and quirks of our
Trade Winds and could exploit nuances of the wind

currents while the inept imported force sat idle at their machines.

The company had no choice but to pay him and his fellow locals—since he'd shared his secrets with them—for their superior production. It was now three months since M's funeral.

Plunger guarded memories of M's enduring smile with those perfectly even teeth, but thought sadly of a close relative leading the family patriarch towards the ferry for his last boat ride even as "all concerned" witnessed sadly the spiraling neglect and eventual demolition of a bountiful life gone sour in the face of collateral Development. And, what of the tragic fate resolutely awaiting so many of his cohorts?

FAULTS N'
FIXES:
TENNIS BIZNIS

The Bigger Fix

Plunger often chides himself for his persistent and reckless urge to be "the fixer." Four days into this year's French Open, of which, this time, he'd not even seen a single match on t-v, due to his involvement in a summer institute on leadership, he seemed to be headed smack into a tennis-related fixing event.

And, as he starts retracing his steps, instead of completing his departure from the Courts this evening, he is having misgivings. In the back of his mind is the piece of folk wisdom passed on to him by some elder that warns against retracing your steps to correct an oversight! "You've gone past the problem! Leave well alone! Never retreat!"

Yet, this is precisely what he was doing! He'd returned to the bulletin board where the sign-up sheet for the upcoming "open doubles tournament" was posted.

Damn, just one day to go and there were only three teams signed up! The club would be forced, very likely, to cancel yet another tournament within twenty-four hours!

He could fix that!

So, he called out to his cousin and occasional partner, sitting in the bleachers next to the far court: "B, what do you say? I sign us up to play! Think you're up to it?"

"Sure! Why not!" With nonchalance, but decidedly not "no." In other words, the way he normally reacts to Plunger's half-baked, off-the-cuff suggestions. B is most likely thinking: "Here we go again! The man, at seventy-odd and overweight, can no longer run after a ball, and I am not much better! And this is an open tournament! OPEN, it says on the board, big and broad! When's he going to quit? So, we won the consolation match twice in a row— some years ago! Not last year, nor year before! Anyway…maybe this tournament will decide it for him!"

What Plunger hadn't counted on was the series of extra contingencies in his everyday program— including some especially pressing ones in the summer program!

Like, in his custodial role as one of the institute's directors, his 24/7 availability responsibility for the students, but especially for a certain emotionally fragile but feisty young woman from the neighboring island who complained of breaking out in rashes. Or the flaring up of his stroke-struck younger brother's cellulitis to the point where he would be dispatched to find a giant cabbage! Brief, the signing-up of their lame and decrepit team to play in the tournament, as the tennis literate reader would have surmised by now, was a "fix," because their names on the list would serve as bait! Yeah, but bait for whom? Li'l fish and Big fish alike; the timid and the braggart!

In fact, it might even rid the club of—or at least silence for a while—some disruptive elements who could eventually become threats to the established order! Plunger would hope not to be held responsible for any of the ramifications from his action. If worse came to worse, at least a majority plus one of the unintended consequences, he felt certain, could be categorized as collateral cures. (Well, if we accept the notion of collateral damage, why not its corollary?)

The following morning, Plunger checked the list, and it was clear the bait had been bitten into. Repeatedly and exponentially! For where there had been just three competing teams, there were now twelve! A decent number for the draw in an open tournament in our parts!

But then, late that evening his cell phone rang.

It was B, his cousin and partner. Armed with a flashlight, he was, he informed Plunger, standing in front of the bulletin board at the club. He'd scrutinized the draw, and he couldn't believe his eyes! "For the fourth time in a row, they matched us against the number one seeds in the tournament!"

"Luck of the draw!" Plunger was tempted to say, but the anger in B's voice constrained him to a simple: "Uhh!"

"The draw is fixed, I tell you! Twice, you wonder, three, four times? You need to see this thing, Plunger!"

"Yeah! But not tonight, with a flashlight! My sight isn't that good!"

The following morning Plunger again approached the bulletin board, this time to study the draw. Indeed, there was something suspicious about it. The only team that could be judged closer to a quick exit in this tournament was the one consisting of—believe it or not— the two guys who had signed the sheet individually first and second, each seeking a partner.

They were placed on an extra column! The thirteenth team! You could say, they would be playing a qualifying round. "And that is not our fate!" Plunger said to himself. So what were we complaining about?

But, then again, there was something fishy about this whole business. The number one seeded team, was headed by the club member who had made the draw—at home and behind closed doors. All this, after this club official had assured one and all that he would not be entering the tournament, since he had Guard duty that weekend!

Yeah, Plunger surmised: His own "fix" was no match for the Big Fix! Which is another way of saying: The elder was right! "Young man, learn to walk around the gaping hole!"

The reader will not be surprised to learn that: Plunger and B were soundly trounced by their repeat nemesis opponents. But, then: this team that had signed up for this open, secure in the belief that their ride to the trophy would be a cakewalk, ran smack into the team led by "The Ultimate Club Fixer" in the finals and ended up dubbed simply "finalists."

Winning doesn't count…, but again

Who, as a sportsman, hasn't heard the cliché, "You play with the hand you're dealt? Then you do your best and forget the rest!" Then, again, who hasn't heard the boast from an adult playmate: "I don't play—like certain people—to win; winning isn't important to me!"

With pairings for doubles tennis, it can be decidedly more complicated than these kinds of boasts! The formula for success—or at least for an outcome that won't leave you afterwards seething and stewing in your cowardice-driven despair—could hinge on many more factors than those that come with a simply lousy crap shoot—or the surface composure of your partner.

At least, that's the way Plunger looks back on how matters developed the other night between him and his regular partner. To be more accurate, one would say "how things did not turn out," or one might look only at the few words passed between the partners at the beginning and end of their time on the courts, and reflect on the nature of their partnership! (Lest the reader start suspecting fireworks between the two principals, it should be noted that it is a third party that drew the anger of Plunger's regular partner, Hank; it was the latter's partner for the night, Jeff!)

How did this pairing take place to begin with? (First, it should be known that Plunger and Hank, on the strength of a couple of trophies for Senior Family Doubles—though one of them was in a consolation match, which causes some snickering at the Club—have been ordained "partners" by their cohorts. Last night, though, Plunger merely arrived at the courts just after a match had finished, and the two teams for the next game had already been sent out on the courts.

Knowing something about the skills of all four players, Plunger found the pairings interesting. Let's see, Wally is a lefty, like Hank—and something of his apprentice, having also come into the game late, in this case, from Track and Field. (Hank comes to the game from Baseball, and carries the nickname because local fans saw a likeness in his power at the plate to another "Big H".)

Anyway, tonight, instead of playing safely under Hank's wings, Wally is across the net, partner to Dan, a consummate, wiry pouncer with a frying-pan grip. And, this leaves our Hank (Plunger's regular team-mate) with unpredictable Jeff for a partner.

On the face of it, this should not be a brainer! For, Hank's mantra, in relaxed moments, as he has uttered to Plunger any number of times, is: "Winning is no big thing with me. I play for the fun!" He mutters this snidely when making comparisons with Benny with the ballet-antics forehand and extreme dexterity brought to Tennis from Ping-Pong in which he was an island champion back home and "back when."

"Look at him!" Hank will hiss, after Benny has deftly passed him down the line, from the back court at that, "Anything to win! Isn't this supposed to be a friendly game? You tell me!" All of this only to make note that Hank likes to emphasize that it's not about winning!

Does he know that his idealism will be severely tested this evening? Plunger suspects this, because Hank has said to him more than once: "I just can't stand Jeff's way of playing!" And he has a lot of company! Except when Jeff's game is clicking, and he's making all those impossible insane shots that redound to your team's winning score! For, if across the net, the one guy is wiry and holds the racket like you would a skillet (which presents the opposing player with numerous spinning challenges!), on Hank's side tonight, one finds this highly mobile spark plug, who cuts, then takes risky shots that get plastered, but, who also, should the incoming shot fall in his wheelhouse, meaning from chest level to just above the eyes, it's like the racket in his hands becomes a spear, he kneels low and powers the missile back: at your belly button, your foot, or even your face, as his fancy seems to dictate. "You just don't know what's about to happen when this man's racquet and a tennis ball connect!" Hank complains whenever Jeff is supposedly out of hearing range, not realizing that his tenor voice carries hundreds of feet, especially when he is complaining.

Hank doesn't just complain vocally about things you, as a partner do wrong, he complains with his eyes and pained grimaces.

As Plunger observes the progress of match across

the chain-link fence, he's feeling luckier by the moment, for arriving late and missing the cut! For, Jeff is not clicking too well tonight, which Plunger feels might also have been his own fate on this occasion. And Hank is slouching ever more gravely as the games go by. His mobility is already well known to be very limited, but "Damnit, when I clobber a ball," which he does as long as he can reach it, as is also well known, "and the guy on the other side just manages to pop up a ball in your face, you smash and put away, not this nonsense dribbler that any hacker could run down and put away!"

It seems to be happening a lot, and Hank has already smashed a couple of balls against the back fence in disgust.

When it is all over, the players have shook hands gallantly, and the two right-handers from opposite sides of the court have each departed in his own direction, Hank sits around on the courtside bench to mull it over with his companion southpaw apprentice Wally, who tonight opposed and defeated him. (One could imagine that there were a few provisos and adumbrations made to lessons offered in the past!)

When Wally has to leave due to a commitment made to a family member, Plunger invites his old partner Hank to hit a few balls; it's refreshing returning balls from a solid hitter who is letting off some pent up steam! The Jeff business is still on Hank's mind. "I tell you, I can't stand playing with the guy! Look at the guy good, when he's playing against you! He'll drive the ball to take out your eyes. The man is now on your side, it's a different story. A bunch of weak dribblers or pop-ups!" *But, those weak shots, Plunger wants to tell Hank, happen when the ball comes higher or lower than his wheelhouse. He tries to play it safe, for fear of upsetting you!* But Plunger doesn't dare utter the advice. Besides he wouldn't be heard anyway. For Hank has ratcheted his remarks up to analysis.

"Why this man has to always line up himself to be on my side whenever people are organizing doubles? But I know the answer! Jeff cannot deal with my serve; doesn't want to have to deal with it. So, the coward that he is, he chooses me as his partner!" *But, nothing says you're obligated,* Plunger is thinking. Again he withholds his opinion. At the same time, he's wondering if Jeff, having, in the past, overheard the behind-the-back snippets Hank throws his way, hasn't been proactive in positioning himself for the doubles pairings, in order to bring grief to Hank.

"Do you know, that these guys had us five-zip, before I won that game to make it five-one; then we broke Wally, so it ended up six-two!"

So…Plunger is left to wonder about Hank's time-worn boast: "Winning means nothing to me! I'm not like some people."

"Incense, defile no more these Courts!"

It's a sport, here in the West Indies, you'll see engaging adolescent boys, on almost every wharf or waterfront, at some time or another.

They've been at it since wharves first appeared on our shorelines. First, they'll coax or cajole him towards the brink, next, they'll either gang up or sneak up on the distracted, inattentive, weaker or hapless chum and toss him off the pier into the deep water.

Shocked, he is left to fend for himself. As a spectator, you too are shocked and frightened for the safety of the boy overboard. Not to worry! The gang knows their victim will make it to shore, even if it's with two mouthfuls of seawater in his throat and halfway down into his lungs.

Concerned? Save your worries for the adults—and even the elderly—who get tossed into the deep water (or the ring) by adult, seasoned pranksters!

Plunger got to the University Tennis Courts that

evening and exited his aging Corolla just as a doubles set drew to a close. He popped the trunk, grabbed his racket and a can of balls and headed for the stands.

"No, Doc! Don't sit! You're next! We've got three men waiting; you'll make the fourth!"

"Gentlemen, my plan for now is to observe your fine play, see what techniques I might pick up…"

"No, no, no, Doc! You're up; the guys are waiting!"

"Ok, Ok! So, who is going to…?

"I'll carry you," Declared Damien, a tad self-sacrificially. His skinny, wiry frame is a good match for his comically wily and totally unorthodox tactics. (No amount of ridicule poured on him for his "frying-pan" grip has convinced him to hold the racket more respectfully!) Yet, he is lightening fast; fleet of foot, in fact!

And, who are their opponents? Plunger first surveys the nearby courtside bench. Of the two men sitting there, licking their wounds from the recent trouncing they'd received, the most noteworthy was the least competent tennis-wise.

Alfred came into the game less than a year ago, from Cricket. Like so many cricketers, he is strong on the half-volley. He also tracks ground strokes well and runs efficiently to catch up with the ball. His serve is inconsistent—especially when his ambition and self-consciousness kick in. The biggest shortcoming he possesses is a forehand without extension.

"Extend, Al! EXTEND!" In how many different voices and how many times, has it been shouted at him, during practice sessions and now even during games! Alfred does it his own way, and now he is getting better at what he does poorly! Which is now earning him the indifference, if not the plain contempt, of past well-wishers. (For, no matter how magnanimous, it is disheartening to see someone get better and be more successful with tools that you despise!)

All of this to say that this was the Alfred that was assigned to the aging and hardly mobile Plunger by the bench-warming matchmakers— not the least of which was one of the players, nicknamed Salo, rising to take one of the slots across the net for tonight's doubles!

That was a week ago! What was one to do? Tennis life is tough like that at times. Far simpler to deal with the deck you're dealt! Dodging an assigned partner can lead to bruised egos and enemies for life!

Yet, Plunger is keenly aware that his arrival at the courts at that precise moment last week was the match the fellows needed to ignite their pent-up mischief!

As for tonight, much of what lies ahead promises to be the same thing. However, the team on the opposite side of the net consists of a solid conventional player and precisely the mischievous matchmaker of last week, the man now taking to the court. He is of special interest to Plunger! Especially because of a remark he'd clearly heard him making as Plunger and his inexperienced partner, last week, were passing close by on the first changeover, after a particularly hard fought first game, to boot!

As if it didn't suffice to set up a totally lopsided match and guarantee failure for Plunger and partner, Salo chose his words carefully, as they were passing nearby, in pointedly muttering an adage to the effect that small dogs often must learn the hard way the consequences of trying to swallow large bones! This time, a half hour later, it's all over!

Plunger and his wiry, unpredictable but fast and agile partner, with trip-hammer intensity and voracity have befuddled, overwhelmed and pummeled their opponents convincingly by a score of 6-2.

Plunger believes that the win came about through, first of all, the overconfidence and even contempt of the weaker one of their opponents, the fellow they call Salo! Added to this was an overdrive turbo output whipped by pent-up and dramatically released urges linked to scores of provocations and insults that at once defile and enchant the premises!

On pelting rocks and batting balls

A friend of Plunger remembers that a big commotion broke out in her neighborhood one day. A man of reasonably normal appearance and of obvious robust health was seen pelting good sized rocks at his lawnmower. While doing this, he was shouting loudly some expressions that could not be deciphered by the spectators who'd gathered:

"Ga-ba-bra-bra-ma-ma-dra-dra-tra-tra…," and so on it went. Several persons approached the man to request he explain his action and his anger. The high-pitched gibberish didn't cease; nor did the rock pelting.

Then a neighborhood lady of about the man's age stepped forward, proclaimed that she knew the man from childhood, and told all concerned that the man was without speech.

"Cyan't talk, you say? But, how's that? He's going through all the motion of a talking man, spacing what he's saying and raising and lowering his voice even. We just cannot understand him. It's like when a child is scared stiff and can't get the words out!" a male spectator who looked like a lay preacher offered.

"You hit the nail on the head," the lady announced. "As a boy, he talked like any other person. Then, he and a friend got it in their head one night to visit the cemetery, they said, to chase the jumbies out once and for all. Well, they heard a rustling of leaves, and the buddy took off. This one, on the other hand, turned around to look. Only to see the jumbie smack in front of him! Fright seized him, and from that day to this, he's never been heard to say a word anybody could understand!"

When Plunger had heard this account of the angry man without speech, he reflected back on what he'd said to his friend that stimulated her to tell this story to him. He didn't have to think back too far! He'd just moments before related to her the incident that took place at the public courts at the end of a doubles match the night before. The mixed team on the near court was heading through the west gate and towards the stands where Plunger would commend them on their play, though they had lost! Then the male player—they called him

Hank for the power he possessed as a batsman in
baseball—exploded with a loud injunction about his
right to say whatever he had to say. Now, listen in
carefully, and you'll hear Nellie, for that's his
partner's name, almost whispering to him: "But the
only thing I was saying to you, Hank, is not to
worry about the li'l miss-hit; we could do it. Just
urging you on, that's all I was doing!" "There you
go, again!" Now Hank's voice is rising to a feverish
pitch. "Did I tell you I was worrying about
anything, Did I? Tell me! Don't I have a right to get
pissed with myself over crap that I do on the court?
How do you get into it? Tell me!"

"Hank, you're taking it the wrong way! I was just…"

"You were just, you were just! Do I need you or
anybody saying anything to me the second I get
pissed over crap I myself did? It's disgusting! 'Don't
worry, Hank! Forget it, Hank!' Don't you and the
whole stands hear others shouting out their name
over errors they make? Do I say anything to you
when you hit the ball against the fence?"

By now the partners were within range of Plunger
in the stands and Nellie was searching fans' faces

for back-up in the face of this fury.

Plunger managed to utter, "Hank, man. . .!" In a flash, the outburst came his way. "And now, everybody must jump on me! Over what? Me criticizing MYSELF!"

This was the incident that resulted in Plunger hearing about the speechless angry man. The reader will query: What's the lesson in linking the two stories? How about some vague linkage to "Communication!"

To Hank's credit later in the evening, he and Plunger were the last two to leave the premises, and they calmly chatted about another matter. Inevitably, however the chat drifted to the discord between him and his partner. Declaring, "You'll probably fly off the handle when I tell you..." was the way Plunger "seguayed" into the subject.

And they made enough headway for him to gain a concession that the conduct in question, in the context of a doubles match, could easily signal to the opposing players that "these guys aren't together! Let's move in for the kill!"

Even conceding this to be the case, Hank maintains that his right to kick his own butt is inviolate! To this day, Plunger is not sure which is more futile: coming to understand the man without speech noisily pelting rocks at a dumb lawn mower, or getting this baseball star-turned tennis player to see the game the way tennis players generally see it. He suspects the latter to be more hopeless. For, the first of these individuals could just possibly be trying to say something good to himself and the world in his speechless tirade. The latter seems forever doomed to beat himself down, whenever he trips.

MOTHERS
AND SONS

X-treme Prodigal Groom-Son

Today—as she gracefully advances into her late seventies—she is able to laugh about the incident, but does not deny that had one little detail been different she might still at this time be locked behind bars, second guessing the snap decision to so violently take her son's life.

It started when the young man returned from University and introduced to her and her husband the young woman he proposed to wed, whom they could only view as the product of the class of people who had oppressed and exploited them and theirs.

"Do what suits you," she'd advised the young man as soon as she was able to break him loose from the foreign damsel, "but you can forget about any gift from me that might one day end up in the hands of her and her people!"

There was a principle to uphold, and nothing more! As if to prove the purity of her scruples, the local woman took steps to provide an impeccable cultural experience for her son's fiancée.

When it was known that the latter would be leaving the island—after this first visit—in a few days, the woman came up with the idea of a superb cultural treat. She recalled that in the neighborhood there was a candy maker who went unmatched in the making and presenting of sweets of the highest quality and beauty. Her son was an absolute fanatic of these treats, as was evident every time he returned home and beseeched his mother to secure a batch of those and no other sweets. So, what better idea than to place an order and to properly present the candies to their guest! This was done with suitable pomp, in a well chosen vessel set on a finely embroidered caster.

As things would happen, the young couple was standing together as the delivery was being made. To the mother's total surprise, her son asked: "What is that?"

With this, the mother did a 180 degree turn, rushed down the stairs to her car, opened the trunk, pulled out the gun she found there, took dead aim on her son, then apprised him of how lucky he was that this was only a popgun. "If this was a real gun, you would be a dead man in seconds!" she declared.

Patsy's Legacy of Turmoil

Patsy's second son, B, enters his line of vision as, sitting on his front porch, he sips on his morning cup of coffee. It's a Saturday morning, and he's got a bucket in one hand and a broom in the other. From the bandstand to the bayside, he's on the last lap of his weekly self-imposed task of collecting trash and litter on the streets of our small island community. And what better time than a Saturday morning— given the savagery and unbridled recklessness of the Friday night street jams of the younger crowd, bolstered by the legions of American college Spring-breakers!

For, on this circuit alone, in their town there are two well established old line churches, and tomorrow, Sunday, their staid and proper congregants (repentant miscreants, as some of them are!)— imbued with the "Cleanliness/Godliness" doctrine—are likely to be particularly critical about the town's appearance as they transit to and from worship!

One would say B honors the nobler side of his late

mother's memory! Not that there was an ignoble side! But those in attendance at her funeral, a few months ago, on her home island—and a substantial multitude of locals traveled by several boats from neighboring islands to be there—[How could you not do so after the same son met you and said, in one breath: "Patsy burying next Saturday, back home! You coming, right?"] would bear testimony that Patsy constituted single-handedly her own bundle of cascading and highly contagious turmoil!

In this writer's time he has attended a number of huge funerals, with crowds overflowing out of the church and around the block, but never at one of these blockbuster funerals has he heard so much in the way of eulogies and testimonials that could fill the sanctuary with such lusty laughter and gaiety as that occasioned by the relates of the departed's mischief and its effect on a community! One was left with the impression that, at the wake the night or two before, the best griots from the island's neighboring communities had converged and, after endless relates about Patsy and her impishness, which in turn spawned other relates on long deceased women of similar penchants and proclivities, a truce was declared that she was "The

Queen of Melee Women!"

"Hey, what's up?" he calls out, when Patsy's son is facing him, twenty-five feet away, across the oleander hedge he planted as a screen from the street's errant eyes and dust. His simple query, he well knows, could open the door to an extended blow-by-blow treatise on much that needs fixing in their lives, their Economics and their Community. But, what the heck! He has a few minutes to burn. (Besides, he's been asked to scout around for a good candidate as a running mate for their chief political officer.)

"Nothing much, Doc! Staying out of trouble."
"That's not hard for you. You're always busy! By the way, PN is looking for help with his campaign."
B sets down his bucket and broom, turns around and makes his way down the steps into his yard.

"Funny you mention PN, Doc! The man walked up to me in the airport the other day and started a conversation on what needs to change around here. Now, Doc, you know I keep my distance from politicians and big shots. . .!"

"But, I just told you: the man is in search of a running mate!"

"Yeah, but Doc, it's not about what we need to change in Public Policy that we have to address right now! It's what we got to do in the privacy of our families that needs our pressing attention. And, when I say pressing, I mean real pressing, Doc!" His high pitched voice has risen an octave, and "Doc" knows he's in for it!

"Doc, take me, Patsy and my younger brother! You know who stuck with Patsy all these years, while every Saturday, doing what I'm doing with the kids, and the difference between that and the action of the one of us who swaggers around this town like Mr. Big!—when he chooses to show his face!" And now he sticks his hands in his pants pockets and does a take on his younger, taller brother, puffed up to the maximum. "Who built the concrete house for his mother," he continues, "while she worked as a maid for the Man! I don't need to continue this, Doc! Just to tell you how Patsy dealt with us two!

"Doc, I would listen as my mother said to me more that once: 'B, I don't know what I would do without you! Having you is like having ten soldiers guarding my back!'

"But a few minutes later the phone would ring. It would be my brother calling from the States. She would take the phone and start a conversation with him: 'W, when are you coming home, Boy? ...I don't know if I go last that long! This brother o' yours is making life so miserable for me. I believe he wants to kill me off!'

"That's why, I say, Doc. It's in the privacy of the family that we've got to start fixing what's wrong around here! Doc, I'm not going to take up anymore of your time! But, I'll tell you one thing, Doc: in this matter between my big shot brother and me about property, the Courts will have to settle it!"

And, with that, Patsy's son picks up his bucket and broom and heads around the corner towards the bayside, in all likelihood, to check on the coconut slips he planted for the enjoyment of future generations.

P wept over Milagro's tithing miracle boy child!

While waiting for the late ferry for the trip back home, Plunger and P, who ran the dockside meal wagon, would have these chats. In point of fact, P would relate events, adventures and escapades that defined the special person he knew himself to be. Plunger mostly listened, but sometimes stoked the chat with a raised eyebrow or a query of disbelief.

This time it had to do with a visit from his son, who lived in the States, accompanied by his wife and children.

As things would have it, P was attending to a health matter when the folks arrived. For a week to ten days P had stayed home, forgotten about his customers at the ferry dock, and rested a troublesome knee.

During this break his visiting son Buddy, made him gifts of two hundred dollars on arriving in the islands and another hundred before departing. But what touched P the most was the warm prepared food he brought every day.

So, P ate well, healed, reflected . . . and wept.

If this son of P was something of an accident from the get go, his survival and growth into the strapping hulk he was today was a miracle.
P tells of the two attractive sisters, one of whom gave birth to, later abandoned, then returned to intervene in the raising of his son. (Yes, it sounds convoluted, but stories like these are not rare in our islands!) He'd seen the sisters exploited and toyed with by any number of the more "up and standing" local men. What began, then, as a goodwill offer of shelter from this exploitation to one of the sisters, the one named Milagro, turned into a relationship of some duration.

She bore him a child, then a second and a third.

"I am the one that brought up those children. Not their mother, not their grandmother."
"Not even their grandmother?"

"She was too busy keeping house for the children of that bunch of spree boys, including some that was good friends with your father."

Plunger considers this linkage for the briefest of moments then decides he and P know each other well enough that the little dig could mean a lot but could also mean nothing.

P receives word from his cousins in Tortola that a child he had fathered on that island was discovered in a house where it had been left three days earlier while the mother came to St. Thomas. The child's belly was bloated and his eyes were bulging. He has the child brought to St. Thomas.

Now commences a tug-of-war between P and his sister over the little boy. P establishes the rule that only the mother must groom the child because he doesn't like what the others would do with the boy's hair. "Black people like to make a bunch of divisions and rows and things like that!" And Pilot feels his child has smooth hair. "Good hair!"

It's that simple!

P's sister overhears his instruction to the child's somewhat wayward mother. As a blood aunt to the child she no doubt considered herself having a proprietary interest! For, on another occasion P has declared to Plunger that he fathered numberless children, many on that neighboring island, where, as a small boat skipper and deliverer of foodstuff and dry goods from a supplier on our island, he enjoyed many favors of the flesh! Who knows how many of these ended up on their aunt's door step. This aunt would lure the child's mother to her place, which was not too difficult, since the two were drinking partners. P came looking for his boy, saw the results in the women's (evidently) negotiated hairstyling, and Hell broke loose!

The long and short of it is: he finds himself brought before the District Court judge by his sister who accuses him of trying to run her over with his truck on at least three occasions at three different locations. P never really owns up to having done any such act in his account to Plunger, but the latter has reason to believe, from what was said before, that the man was that angry over the "picky-haired look" on his pride and joy. (Hadn't P once told him that stud or no stud, he was not crazy about frolicking with women of his race, since the bristle was too hard on him!!!)

That he tried to maim his sibling over her disfiguring his child was a strong probability! The judge, in any case—who knew and sympathized with P—would find the accusations groundless, especially since the sister's witnesses never showed up. He would warn P's sister not to try any such "cat-an'-bull" story again before the Court if she didn't want to receive half of the penalty she was here seeking for her brother.

The judge then turns and cross examines the boy: "Do you know who this person is? Yes? He is your father? OK. One day you'll be a man. You must never forget what your father did for you. If you earn something in life, give half of it to your father. Do you understand?"

P told Plunger that he sat at home ate his food, rested his bad knee, slept and woke up... and cried, when he thought back to all these things.

COCKY GAMES
FOR ALL AGES

Laiyo our fledgling Sexual Griot and Tutor

Let's see! Who else in this class of '55 remembers it the way I do: That day, Laiyo had news for the boys in Ms. Francis' 8th grade homeroom class. To wit, the afternoon before he'd been given a proper cut-assing by Mr. S. the principal. So what else is new, one of the less impressed asked (speaking up for the rest of us). Come on, Laiyo, you said news!

Laiyo brushed aside the snide riposte, as was his habit, and went to the heart of the flogging event.

Igualda had made it happen! Igualda, the new female in our class. From Puerto Rico, much more developed than the others and possessing only a few words in English and our English Creole.

Ah! But it's her special way of rolling them off her tongue! And Laiyo had a special predisposition and predilection for provocative sounds! Which is to say, he could imitate them to a "t". And the string of mischief he fabricated with these purloined sounds was endless! Whether, the buzz of a mosquito in a neighbor's ear, during some teacher's absolutely essential diatribe, a resounding belch during some classmate's well rehearsed and highly valued recital, or a hallway monitor's fire evacuation announcement, in the closing moments of a school-wide assembly.

Laiyo's specialty, however, were sounds related to—or, one might say, derived from—coupling activities, in nature at large. Wasn't it Laiyo that broke the code for us of the yard cock bent on another conquest? "Rrrr! Kuk, kuk, kuk! Rrrr!" he would inform us, "in fowl language, that only means: 'Look in meh pocket! Yo' go fine a quarta!'"

"So, wha happen den?" Some dimwit would ask. "Idiot! De hen come closa to look! De nex' t'ing, he jump on her, an' dat takes care of dat!"

Never mind his story about the alley cats and their carryings-on, which the naïve among us believed had to do with cats fighting! But, by far the best of his acts was when he brought forth the late night sounds from his parents' bedroom. Between the woman's plea—sometimes for mercy, other times for more—and the "skwish-skwash" of the metal bedstead, it was a full-blown concert!

"Laadyogokillme!   Laadamercy!   Laadyokillme! Laadyokillme! Laaddoit" went his grand finale.

So, what was yesterday's flogging from the principal all about?

Igualda, the well-developed girl from the island down west, had reported Laiyo to the principal!

Reported him for what?

Let Laiyo tell it in his own words: "De gyurl went straight to Mr. S. office and say to him: 'Laiyonel say he want to skeeruu me!'"

"An' wha happen?"

"Meh son!!! De man put a beatin' on me, an' I bawl out: 'Lawdyo go killme! Lawdyo go Killme!'"

"Jus' like?"

"Jus' like! Aiie! Aiie! Aiie!"

"OK, Laiyo! Nex' time when yo' come wid news, see if we could report it widout makin' us chase de chil'ren from de room!"

Rubio's sojourn at the
Koq-Comfort Roost

What was Mano's 3-Star Koq-Comfort Roost? It was, first and foremost, the complete antithesis of today's labor intensive egg-producing fowl hutch. It was, in fact, Mano's monument of defiance against the worst atrocities Man deftly commits daily against the most domesticated of winged creatures.

Mano, having grown up on a poultry farm, knowing the ins and outs of that industry from pillar to post, and also understanding the irrefutable dictates of the profit-motive, had one day decided to cast his hard earned pearls to the betterment of the male members of Man's closest feathered friend and food supplier!

Who was Rubio? Read on!

Who was "at-risk Happy?" The name says a lot.

When streetman "at-risk-Happy" decided to go seek lodging for Rubio, his fighting cock, at Mano's 3-star Koq-Comfort Roost, it did not go un-noticed

by the Sport's hoi-polloi on our island. For, at the
upper end—those who considered the Sport the
rightful property only of the indolent affluent—
Happy's petition was plainly outrageous and
"Whatever you do," was their directive to
Management of Mano's Comfort Roost, "make sure
you don't lodge raggedy Happy stinking, pip-
infected cock within a hundred yards of any of
mine!" At the other end of the spectrum, were
those who shrugged at Happy's uppity deed, while
remarking, "De man ain' got de 'p' of a pot to piss
in!"

The contempt was more a product of some rapidly
changing practices and outside social influences in
our small island than a result of unsavory acts by
Happy. By then we were a small circle of island
elders who knew the distance Happy had traveled
from his first appearance in our community. (This is
not to say that Happy had scaled the ranks to now
be considered "Somebody."!)

When we, lately of the generation of elders, first
knew of him on the island, he was known as the at-
risk nephew of a tambourine-banging, portly
woman missionary, she being the sidekick of the

late-life bride-to-be of one of the town's main grocers, boat captain and fisherman.

The physically more diminutive member of this female missionary partnership, it would later appear to us, was the engine of Happy's entry into our community. For, while it was his hefty and solidly-built aunt of the drab grey frock and brimmed straw hat who first caught your attention through her thunderous country alto voice and energetic beating of the tambourine, her smaller companion's mostly covert yet snappy intrusions during their curbside revival crusades left no doubt about her own innate capacity for more dervish antics in the wider worldly context. All of this is by way of explaining why it was no surprise, with the passage of time, to learn that Captain Wally's apparent Christian-motivated generosity in lodging the trio downstairs of his newly constructed two-storey edifice—the only legitimate one of such impressive signature on the island, apart from the Administrator's office and residence—was the snare with which he would soon snap up the smaller exotic prey.

So, in time Wally would wed the petite and energetic

clear-skinned middle-aged woman, and Happy and aunt, now suddenly disposable, she first then he would vanish from our community.

It was in the period following their eviction from Captain Wally's downstairs and after his aunt's departure from the island that Happy entrenched himself further as a street-survivor. "Entrench" might be too strong! For in that time frame that preceded the ostentatious American charities, a young man about town of Happy's origins and upbringing dared not harbor dreams of fitting in among our small sector of "Big People."

His art of survival depended on the delicate trick of balancing personal utility and discreet obscurity. From our earliest youth we are inculcated with the mandate that some people are to be seen and not heard. Happy survived by at times even eclipsing himself! Today, we suppose, the appropriate word would be, at least occasionally: "Whipping Boy" or a "Gofer."

He knew where to be when he needed to be there! In fact, one night he had a terrifying lesson in what happens when one approaches too close to the edge in dealings with our Big People. It was the opening night of the first Carnival on our big sister island of St. Thomas. Two boatloads of festival-goers from our cousin island of Tortola had set sail earlier that day for our neighboring shores. Off the west end of our island, which can be viewed as mid-point betwixt the two larger islands (the one of embarkation and the one of debarkation in this case), the boats had been becalmed.

For such emergencies those sailboats were equipped with a pair of large and weighty oars. Who knows whether manning the latter would contribute to the mood among the crew when the boats finally docked in our harbor and the decision was made for passengers and crew to come ashore and stretch!

The only bar in this part of the island at the time was run by a son of the same Captain Wally, and the Big People of our island, who did not see any need to travel to St. Thomas for fun, were out doing some merry-making of their own that night at the bar. Happy was close enough to benefit from a shot of rum literally shoved along the counter his way from time to time, in exchange for running some simple errand.

Our becalmed mariners, including the women travelers, headed for the bar as a place for replenishments and whatever. In no time the two groups of clients were occupying the limited space of the little combination bar and grocery store, each group to its side.

Business could not have been better for Skipper Wally's son that night…till someone from the local side made a fresh remark to one of the ladies in the visitors' group. Their leader stepped forward and wanted to know who had insulted the lady. Of one accord, the Big People—finding themselves outnumbered in their own home bar, but no doubt remembering Happy's reputed skills as a boxer— offered him up as the culprit.

In the pandemonium that followed, which spilled over into the street, little Happy found himself properly pummeled by a boatman twice his size. The distraction, however that his private struggle entailed allowed a retreat into the nearby bushes by the smaller force of our Big People. From those bushes, Happy, when he'd finally escaped from the claws of his heavyweight tormentor, led our forces in that historic pre-Carnival St. John vs. Tortola pitched battle. And it was truly pitched in the sense that stones, bottles, bricks, it took before our visitors retreated to their vessels in our harbor.

After that night Happy disappeared from view. When he re-emerged on our island scene Happy was an older—in fact, visibly aging—man and a wiser one. First of all, the encounter between him and Rubio, the disgraced and much maligned cock, was of general knowledge. The way that encounter took place is discretely codified in the oral lore of our most zealous living Culture gatekeepers.

The eye-witness account we managed to consult commenced with a preamble to the effect that once more Happy was where he needed to be when the great event took place, namely a stone's throw from the pit, in Smith Bay, snoozing away the afternoon by the giant bolder he felt to be home. (As relates to the cockpit's legal status, someone had scribbled in the margin of the document a note (an FYI, in fact) to the effect that one of our best jurists had ferreted out a loophole in legislation on such activities and exchanged the information for questionable political leverage.)

So, Happy's encounter with Rubio, the disgraced fighting cock, took place the very afternoon that the latter's lack of valor in the arena caused his master to tumble into the sandy pit stone-dead. For, in the confusion that ensued, with many of St. Thomas' Big People absconding without winnings and belongings before the inevitable arrival of the forces of law, order and health and brazened ordinary people descending into the very pit to dispute over the money either gained or lost—since not a few claimed that the bet was now off—Rubio, who had only pretended to be mortally wounded, took to his wings, flew through the crowd and never stopped flapping those wings till he had alighted on Happy's sunning boulder!

The encounter between the now aging street warrior and Rubio contained its full dose of inverse manifest destiny. For, once the fighting cock's perceived cowardice in the arena was announced as the cause of his master's fatal attack, he was deemed a cursed reprobate, and the fighting public's edict was for an all-points bounty on Rubio, though among those in pursuit of him some secretly desired to grab him in order to breed a yard of tricky cocks!)

On the other hand, Happy was only recently back on the streets. The long tentacles of the Halt Vagrancy/Loitering Services, steered by the anti-Domestic Violence Society, had in time sniffed him out, after all these years and fallen on him with its full complement of referrals and interventions, with the net results that he'd been placed for a stint in his own flat, furnished with the conveniences. But only for a stint, mind you, for the machinations by which the property containing his flat had been hastily acquired for the homeless, were soon under the interested scrutiny of the islands' latest upscale developers. Upon nullification of the previous sale, and Happy, his kit and caboodle, along with his ilk, summarily evicted, the latest in real estate spitfire max-ing was set in motion and the property "flipped" in short order through several cycles, to the joyous chorus of our latest absentee landlords, i.e., fortune-hunters in places like New York, Chicago, Zurich and London.

Now, back in his more familiar haunts, he'd installed himself in this vacant lot whose distinguishing landmark was a giant boulder that he called his "sunning rock." There he would spend the better part of his time philosophizing on the social space that lay between himself, at the one pole, and the rapidly vanishing "Big People" that occupied the opposite end of the continuum. He never failed to recall the pummeling he'd taken from the "junk-of-iron" man from Tortola that pre-Carnival night in the bar on St. John—all over the freshness of one of the island's Big People towards the "sister"— as he now sees her—from the becalmed sailboat. Yet, from the retreat of the bushes across the street, he'd had his moment of heroism in leading the troops of the island's Big People in their rocks-and-bottles pitched battle against the visiting forces. He smiles at the recollection, but then grimaces at the deeper signification of this pitched battle between "island cousins" against the backdrop of his recent eviction to make room for the "flipping" crowd. Below the surface of these ruminations of Happy a new dialogue has recently crept into his consciousness. It has more to do with what he is hearing around him than what he might be verbalizing in his mind.

The giant boulder, at the beginning his exclusive premises, has now become the meeting point for a band of semi-vagrant young people. (It has been rumored that the group viewed Happy and his whereabouts as the perfect shield, from the roving eyes of law enforcement, for their questionable practices, since the world knew him to be harmless and still possessed of a heart of gold.) So, on any clear day Happy's tranquility is invaded by their noisy jousts on cockfighting, dog fighting and other survival enterprises in the underbelly of this community meandering through the throes of overdevelopment.

Happy has no property rights; he does not complain. Nor is he judgmental. He calmly does his own philosophizing and from time to time appropriates some common sense from the noisy verbal confrontations of these young people.

Such was the main train of his thoughts the day Rubio flew out of the cockpit and into his life. And just as abruptly, he made the analysis that this bird deserved his day in Court. The way Happy viewed the matter: Rubio was alive, first and foremost, because he was true to the adage, "He who fights and flies away..." So, it would be hypocritical to consider the red and black cock disgraced and to respect the bounty placed on him. Moreover, from his eavesdropping of the deliberations on cockfighting by the young neighborhood experts, he'd gathered some ideas on how the trainers went about sharpening the fighting proclivities of their cocks: deprivation of sexual favors, followed by lavish rewards after victory; similar machinations over food; even spitting in their faces and the like! Happy came to the conclusion that Rubio needed none of the above, but only the boosting of his self-esteem in order to face up to the fiercest winged foe, in the center and only the center of the arena! A sojourn in Mano's 3-star Comfort Roost was the least he could do for him, beg, steal or borrow!

SEAWARD AND BE DAMNED

Passing muster with Gramps

Now into his early seventies, the first challenge this retired professor of languages regularly faces each morning on coming awake is the choice of his main physical activity for the day. It often comes down to deciding between a couple of sets of doubles tennis or a couple of hours of trolling aboard his Bronze Ruler. The fact that his grandson, a first year aviation student, is visiting from the bigger island doesn't change much. He's gone and gotten him into tennis too, and they make a decent doubles team. And, today the young man has decided he'd like to take to the sea with him.

(And, the young man's mother—his own first daughter—has a way of nudging him concerning his grandfatherly duties: "When they're with you, it's partly so that you can impart to them some of those cultural traditions they won't learn in books, Dad!")

Some years ago he named his boat Bronze Ruler/Règle de Bronze. Before choosing that name, he'd considered calling her Golden Ruler/Règle d'or

II. The "II" business however, would be pompous, he'd quickly concluded. True, two boats before his ownership of this twenty-five foot bronze hulk of a three-decades old Formula he'd proudly named the nineteen-footer then in his possession "The Golden Rule(r)". As for the one between the first Rule(r) and the present boat, she went un-named, and he'd just as soon forget she'd ever existed, since she'd tried to drown him one Friday afternoon as he headed towards the Atlantic side of the barrier cays in search of fry bait!

This afternoon Plunger stands at the water's edge, one boat-length away from the stern of the Ruler (since he anchors her bow seaward), and he bellows orders in his baritone voice to his grandson, the first year University student.

"No! I said: Push down on the button, push the lever a good ways into the forward position. RELEASE, I said, RELEASE the button! Then start! This way she can warm up! You keep stalling, and you will eventually flood the motor..."

"Like this?" the young man yells, over the loud complaint of the racing motor.

"Yes, but pull back on the throttle, before you blow something...Not so suddenly! You've got to apply some TOUCH, man!

"And, when you get the motor idling properly, you need to lower the foot further into the water, go to the bow, loose the anchor rope from the cleat. THEN YOU'VE GOT TO WORK FAST; cast off the anchor rope at the bow, get back to the controls, lower the motor further into the water, back up on the stern anchor, but do so carefully, so you don't pick up the rope with the prop!" [Ayyy! But this young man moves too slow! He's uncomprehending of what the slightest gust of wind can wreak! Especially with those shoals and rocky coastline off to the left! Does he begin to understand the relationship between the ample freeboard the Règle possesses and the effect of a gust of wind against her sides?]

He does not like to discourage, especially with dire comments on the unalterable, Yet, he's tempted to say to him: "Your trouble is, you got into this boat business too late! Like me and tennis! You'll improve with time, but you'll never perform like a natural."

If he does, he'll have to break it out: The way it had been with his own old man and the brothers and cousins. The no-nonsense lessons at a tender age, then placing them at the helm with full control, so that "if anything happens one day…" they would know what to do. And things did happen a couple of times.

Just the other day, in fact, his older brother was reminding him of one of those events. "Remember the silver dinghy?" Of course he did!

Literally, a sea coffin with a one half horsepower Elto "egg beater" propelling it. The boat, barely six-feet in length, violated every principle of sea craft construction, except that it possessed a tapered bow. The bottom was flat, and, atop the four inches or so of decking capping the gunwales on port and starboard sides, was a ledge that rose another three or four inches, all adding to the tipsy nature of some whimsical tinsmith's idea of a sea vessel.

(One day, he recalled, in this same bay, the wake from a larger slow moving boat had capsized the dinghy with his father in it.) "Well, one day," his brother continued the story, "our mother, about to prepare a meal and finding herself without oil to sprinkle on the pitch pine kindling, to start up the coal pot, commanded me to travel in that death trap from Cruz Bay to Caneel and back, to purchase kerosene in the Commissary"

"No kidding! And, you think it was as windy as it is today, GranPa?"

"Maybe more, maybe less. The point is: this mother of ours, who couldn't swim a lick, sent her first son out in the channel—which we called "the Gut" in those days—to brave the elements, on the sole belief that her husband had imparted to the boy how to deal with whatever might befall him! The other time, by then in Trade Wind, the twenty-one footer our dad came to own, late one afternoon the old man had us drop him off on the beach at Great Cruz, so he could go duck hunting in the pond. What he needed was quiet; that is probably why he left us pre-teenagers on the boat. We would wait till he returned to the boat, then head back to Cruz Bay.

"Well…we waited and waited, and it got darker and darker! Then we took turns standing on the cabin and calling 'Daddyyyyy!' Then, all three of us together!

"What had happened to him? Our collective despair and helplessness was not the answer. We held counsel and decided to return to Cruz Bay, to report our experience. We started up Trade Wind, gave her full throttle and headed back to port, in the darkness, navigating around more than one rocky cliff and between two treacherous reefs on the way!

"As we stepped off the boat and rushed to home base to report the mishap, tears streaming down our faces, there burst in our dad to the same place, to report his missing boat with his missing boys!"

Grandpa and grandson are well underway on board the Règle, powered by a 200 hp Evinrude Bombardier; it's the older man's dreamboat since its cabin is recessed into a well that allows him a safe catwalk up to the bow to handle business like casting an anchor and retrieving it. They've exited the harbor, after pulling in at the fuel dock in the creek, where, since the inlet traffic was light and the breeze gentle, the young man was allowed to remain at the helm for maneuvering to the dock. Here again, there are lessons on "if the breeze picks up, and the motor—which you didn't allow to warm up properly—keeps stalling, and you keep overshooting or undershooting the dock going in bow-wise, then change your tactic and back in, after all, the propulsion is in the back of the boat, so you'll have better control that way. Jus' so you'll know how you have to think in adverse conditions!"

So now they're well into the Sound, where the young man appears to be developing a feel for steering through a light wind and chop. Yet, he has to be reminded to keep his eyes on where he's headed. "You seem to 'gyaap' too much; it must come from your great-grand-dad, forever scanning the surroundings. On the sea, it doesn't work that way!"

"But you yourself said he was a real seaman; taught you what you know!"

"Yeah, but traveling at six miles an hour; that was all Trade Wind could do, on a sixteen, then later twenty-five horse power Greymarine four-cylinder flat-head engine! Besides, when we were at the tiller in close quarters, he would always remind us: 'Did you see the sign?'" "Which sign, GrandPa?" "That's exactly what we would ask him, until we caught on. The sign, he said, read 'Keep Out,' because you're in close quarters, and chances are there's a grounding rock or shoal inviting you to disaster."

And then, suddenly: STTTSSSSSTTT!

"Slow down, yeah, pull back on the throttle! A Strike! And come take this pole! I'll take the wheel! Watch your footing, and don't go losing my pole, or our fish…or both!"

"Our?? When did it become "our"?"

[You know? This young man is so full of spunk! This must come from the other side of his bloodline, not ours!] The old man shows him the motion he needs to use to pump the fish back towards the boat. Now, he's alongside; it's a medium sized bonito. Plunger grabs the lead and lifts the six-pounder over the stern and into the boat. "So now you've got a fish. But remember to tell your mom that GranPa gave you the lucky line, and he kept the other one!"

"Luck, you say?? I just did the right thing!"

"Sure, like unable to steer the boat on a beeline, you zigzag all over the place. Couldn't help snagging a bonito quietly going about its own business. Now, we head out through that passage between those two cays. Where do we pass?" "In the middle." "You're getting the idea. Where we are now is on the Caribbean Sea side. We'll be going through to the Atlantic side. And, from what I can see from here, today, you'll witness something that you don't repeat in front of the children!"

"What is that, GranPa?"

"What?"

"What I will see, and what we don't repeat with children present?"

"Ah! Two birds with one stone! Smart alleck! You'll have to wait! And one more thing: if we get another strike, on either pole, no matter how angry the sea, I'm sitting on my hands. You're on your own with both the controls and the pole—like when I'm out here solo!"

"OK, so I'm on the other side of the Sound; came through the narrow channel without any scrapes. Your beloved Règle is safe. Which way do I head now?"

"Just head into the waves; we'll troll our way up to the west end of the Congos; you're heading into a chop, so you'll have to watch the throttle, in case you have to pull back suddenly!"

"A piece of cake!" And they advance towards the Congos, where he often gets a strike. But, no luck this time!

"Now, do a slow turn, so as not to cross the lines, and we head towards Mingo, downwind."

They're now with the swells to their back, and the sea is having its way with the Règle.

"But why all this ziz-zagging, Cyap? And see how that last one almost hit you broadside!"

"I didn't do anything, GranPa. I'm just steering to

where you told me. Oops! This boat is going where it wants! Come back to where I point you!"
"I thought I heard you say a while ago: 'piece of cake'! Son, hopefully one day before you get to my age, you'll learn the genius of Man when he created his first boat. No vessel or vehicle he has built since—whether to travel on land, air or water" was crafted better to communicate with Nature. None! And since you've got so much cheek, head the boat in closer—like 150 feet off the cliffs of Mingo, so the wash from these big waves can hit that wall and come back at you, mixed with what's coming from behind you. What the old folks call: getting it back, belly and side."

Before long the young student pilot is accusing his elder of leading him "into a trap!"

Yet, he proves himself equal to the task. And as they're about to traverse the Bull's Hole to reenter the Caribbean side, what's called Pilsbury Sound, he's asked again about how you traverse an unknown channel for the first time.

"That's easy! Like I said before, you judge for the middle!"

"True, but look carefully ahead, between the two cays! Do you see anything?" "No!...Wait! I see like waves breaking!"

"Good eye! Not in the middle, but close enough to catch you on a calm day, when it's not breaking! So, on the sea, never forget the exception to the rule!"

They troll the inside of the cays and eventually weigh anchor to try some yellowtail fishing in the upper channel. But no sooner was the anchor on the bottom that an innocent looking puffy cloud on the south set its aim on them and instantly lashed them with high blasts of wind and stinging rain.

"That's it!" the elder shouted through the storm. "We haul anchor, and we're out of here! Before I have to answer that question of yours from earlier and tell you what it is that weather beaten fishermen around here have been heard to say after a proper trashing from an ill-tempered Nature."

Which he ended up whispering to the young man: "Boy, today, today, I see meh modda naked!"

Balking Barking Sea Dogs

A close friend wanted to know why they call the cay I was approaching Dog Island! Did it have a history of habitation by dogs, maybe of a special breed? Not having an answer, I could whet her curiosity by relating to her in earnest that as boys my brothers and I—the older one, at that time, just barely a teen and the other, a pre-teen—had often gone there with our dad, maneuvered our boat Trade Wind between the reefs up to the stony bay to land the ole man, so he could hunt ducks and other wetland birds, as was his custom with most of the neighboring cays. And, now, reflecting on it, the approach we'd been taught to the cay was always from the northwest, after skirting Whelk Rocks—which had sunken the sailing vessel Speed out of Cruz Bay with its crew of two non-swimming deckhands who'd managed to survive by tackling pieces of wreckage—before entering the St. James Passage, to slip into the narrow, shoal-filled cove.

Did this instructional lapse on the part of our father have to do with my decision this second day after Christmas when, upon exiting Cruz Bay, I pointed the Ruler's bow towards the head of the Dog? As I started to sense the turbulence of the sea gathering around me, the one dictum of caution the ole man had legated to us from our earliest sailing days buzzed through my consciousness: "Keep out!" It meant, basically, that as you approach a cliff or other outcropping of land, what you see above the water only tells you half the story! What is lurking below sea level in such places is often a malevolent grounding rock. As for the other useful lessons, most came wordlessly through precepts, and when some one of us committed a gaff, the ole man would calmly ask, "Did you see me do that?"

Today's sea was mean-spirited and bore me nor my Bronze Ruler no good will nor warm tidings. What, it seemed to be querying me, are you doing at these head rocks, besides trolling two lines, which, in any case you'll be unable to tend under the respectful conditions I offer you! And those two lines, to boot, that supposedly qualify you as a fisherman—in the eyes of the gullible—which, in the most dire of circumstances, could be your total unraveling, should they foul your prop and kill your forward propulsion in the midst of these high seas!

It's not too late to retreat, fool!

"I'm not too sure it's not too late, Mighty Mastiff of our seas. For, what trails us, to your credit, is no less ferocious than what faces us, as you well know! Good grief! Besides, to attempt a downwind jibe now—as close as we are to these head rocks, is to breach the cardinal rule the ole man laid down to us: 'Keep out! Man made engines, and engines sometimes fail! Then, what do you do???'"

So, I'm torn between your gruff command to retreat and the ole man's words of caution. Besides, as for his guidance, we'd never once seen him retreat from a challenge at sea. It was like this: You don't take it on unless you can handle it! And once you've taken it on, then, see it calmly through to the end! The stiff upper lip is the only way! [But, in the meantime, Mighty Mastiff, would you kindly control your pups? For they nip lustily at the heels of my venerable and worthy Ruler of Bronze! A bit of respect to match what we show you is all I ask on her behalf. We've been through a lot, the Ruler and I, and, were I a less loyal owner, I'll tell you this: her still severely scarred hull would long since have been cluttering our island's public dump.

[Or, worse still, that certain bargain-seeking self-proclaimed sea captain from the larger island, who had made an offer, after learning of her earlier scrape (basically, a submersion by neglect in Cruz Bay), with overzealous volunteer salvagers, would have owned her and promptly set about further defacing her classic flair and lines by radically reducing her sides and freeboard, since he'd declared; "Mr. P., the sides of that boat are too high; that boat could turn over!" It was the threat of this guaranteed disfigurement that froze such negotiations as this presumptuous mariner had initiated with me! So, I beg on her behalf, Great Canine Neptune, call off your pups!]

But then, what do you care about these rambling accounts of me and the Ruler, you Mighty Dog of the Seas, as you first retreat, then muster your forces, and finally thrust forward to pack another vicious thump on the Bronze Ruler's exposed chin!

"Ten to one, 'tis murder!" my tennis buddies would mock, if they were to witness this ambush. "Why go and expose life and limb to such a 'busing' on an angry sea when, at this very moment we could be

trashing your backside more humanely here on our
local courts? The trouble with some of you retirees
is too many options. Just the other day, you had
everyone's eyes popping with that story of how you
and your son-in-law in a stalled 18-ftoot runabout
mid-channel between St. Croix and St. Thomas,
would have been crushed by a mega cruise liner, if
you hadn't insisted his wife return to the house for
the emergency light he'd forgotten, the light that
you would have to wave frantically so the ship could
change course. What is your problem? Some people
hunt bounties! Will you be a hunter of hazards?"

Then, not only it's the exposed chin; it's the fissures,
cracks and creases that the Ruler took, when, after
the mishap in question, and full of water and sand,
the salvage crew insisted on hauling her to dry land
by the force of the all-wheel all-terrain traction of
someone's truck, impatient for the first test of its
much vaunted prowess. These wounds appear to
bleed a sap that draws and excites the dog shark
instinct in you no end, High Priest of the Sea Dogs!
So the waves crest even higher and demand better
than quartering to prevent tumbling. So, at the
wheel, I must edge her more to port while facing,
on starboard, the gaping possibility of us slipping

off the disappearing flank of the preceding swell into the abyss of its trough!

If am to I survive the crossing through this dilemma, something tells me, in order to not tempt you beyond your limits and not overtax the tensile integrity of my humble Ruler, a maneuver will be required of me that hopefully will not dishonor the noble precept of my late father and those that instructed him.

I have resorted to it but once, and that was thirty years ago. And the event happened at a point diagonally opposite to my present position and predicament, namely at the foot of Thatch Island, six miles on a beeline northeast. That was the day I took a puff for a pup, to be more precise, a wind dog for a sea pup! Long before I knew about perfect storms, I'd read in a novel by a man surnamed Trumbull a description of the foxy, ominous and eventually treacherous wind dog.

As we sat, the Missis and I, quietly bottom fishing on the wooden twelve-foot Belly Dancer a hundred and fifty feet off the west of Big Thatch, on that October afternoon when there was a gentle ground swell rolling in from the north, I'd noticed a cloud forming over Li'l Tobago, to the northwest. This grey cloud caught my attention because at about its center, there was this white, cottony puff. Wouldn't it be wonderful if I suddenly were possessed of the talent to paint and could capture this scenery! After all, wasn't it our dad's favorite pastime, on those Sunday afternoons as we returned from trolling at the Tobagos, to draw our attention to the clouds shrouding the setting sun and invite and challenge our animal interpretations of them?

But, before I could fantasize further, a chilling drizzle was upon us, and the wind was bristling, and the gentle ground swell was turning into an angry sea. Conditions changed with such speed as I had never witnessed before, nor have I since. A clear day had turned somber and bluish grey all around us. The light drizzle had transformed into a thousand darts tearing through our light clothing and chilling to the bone; the open hull of the Belly Dancer became a tub from which water had to be bailed every couple of minutes, a task that we took turns at, my spouse and I.

In our mid- thirties at the time, neither of us had

witnessed a true gale or hurricane, but the elders had related to us the sounds that these storms made, and the effect on the trees in their path. On the nearby cay trees were bent back, leaves were flying and the howling was fiercely a sound we'd never heard before.

There came a moment, as dusk started to close in, when it was clear to me that our location was putting us at great risk, and that we needed to pull anchor and head for a sheltered spot. To stay where we were was to risk: a) the swells growing bigger— not to mention the rain intensifying—and eventually swamping or capsizing us, or b) breaking loose from our anchor, possibly where the rope was attached to the cleat, and, until we could get the outboard running, having the wind turn us broadside to the billowing waves to either be swamped or dashed against the nearby cliff.

Having started the 25 horsepower Johnson, I headed into the wind to gain some slack on the anchor rope so I could dislodge and pull it; that maneuver proved futile, and I quickly decided to jettison the anchor rope with a marker.
And now for the crossing! Out here in the passage

the swells were crested hills. One could try to run ahead of them and find one's way across Fungi Hole, the name of the narrow passage between Whistling Island and Mary's Point.

Beyond this passage we would find a sure respite. In short order, however, I knew that I had underestimated the challenge of the crossing. For, quartering the waves behind you and maintaining just enough speed to steer but not so much that you run off a crest only to face its vicious pursuit, is one thing. When you get closer to the cliff, you realize that what is rebounding from it and headed towards your bow is even angrier from its impact with solid, stubborn land mass.

There came that moment of decision when, in the approaching darkness, confronting the huge waves that were roaring back at us from the cliff and the large swell ready to jump our stern, I turned the tiller to port and had a clear vision of us swallowed by the jaws of that swell.
By some miracle I'd managed to get enough of the stern of the Dancer, which, true to its name, tilted up somewhat, unlike our traditional wooden boats, onto the flank of that monster wave, thus sparing

us two-thirds of the wave's dousing, and was subsequently able to set a course along the north side of St. John and into West End, Tortola, remaining throughout in the lee of the storm and having only to deal with the strong current.

I had jibed.

Today, again, I would jibe. Nor dare I make the maneuver too soon! For, that cove just to the leeward of these head rocks, on a normal day, the safe haven after a crossing like this, today would be the bowels of the beast and would churn my Ruler and me before spitting us out in a puree of sinister flotsam.

And, in time, likely with the patience and a bit of wisdom gained from revisiting that scrape with calamity that day thirty years ago off Big Thatch, and now with the distance windward gained away from the rocks at the head of the Dog, I perceived ahead, to port, a trough long enough that I could risk spinning rapidly the steering to bring the ruler around to starboard and coast leeward. Even so, there was a daunting price to pay, for the swell that built up behind just about managed to push the

Ruler's bow below the surface of the long trough ahead. This was when I sprang up from my skipper's seat, to be in optimum control of the Ruler's downwind course—and to render homage both to the challenge of the Dog and the fundamentals of our dad and his forebears in navigation on the high seas.

The Unruly Bronze Ruler

They called my father "Freebird." In fact, that was how he was called by a special and particularly indulgent female cousin of his who usually addressed him this way. And she would greet him with these words each time when we'd crossed the channel in Tradewind and come over to this smaller island on a Sunday hunting or fishing trip.

Was it that daredevil restiveness that "Lanie" saw and admired in him that authorized the name? That, no sooner Tradewind was secured at the dock and greetings exchanged, he'd be off into the wilds to hunt pigeons, doves and ducks on the hilly island or get back on board to go fishing for kings, mackerels and bonitos in our Caribbean and Atlantic waters. What with we, his pre-teen sons, and our local cousins ever on his heels!

And back home, storm clouds would likely be banking for his return! (For the union between our parents saw mostly blustery days!)

"Freebird! Freebird! Hmmph! And you strutting

back home with these children on Sunday at midnight or past, with them having School tomorrow! Who's going to have to shake and wake them, get them dressed, and still have to get herself ready to go off and teach the people's children? Freebird? Hmmph!"

And now, in the image I'm viewing on the screen, I stand knee deep at the water's edge. The video camera is rolling and the interview with me as an elder (during this celebration of Senior Citizens Month) is in progress. I'm running my mouth about how it used to be. I'd stipulated, I would do it for them and for the Culture (the request having come from the Chief Executive's Office), but the package came with the Bronze Ruler!

Who—or What—is the Bronze Ruler? Vessels' names can be deceptive! She (for we'd been taught from earliest childhood to say "she" when referring to a vessel) decidedly doesn't look like a ruler, and the only thing bronze about her is the color of her sides above the waterline, which is more like a beaten-burnished bronze. She is a Formula Sportsman, 24 feet six inches overall, is windshield-less and has major scars and fissures on her bow and at mid-ship, all this due to a misguided salvage effort half a dozen years ago when community do-gooders dragged her sunken carcass back onto the beach, laden with sand and water, rather than first removing and draining the load!

But, she is my ruler. A bit more generational respect and residue of remembrances of my parent's classic donnybrooks and she might be named "Stormy Petrel!"

Never mind!

She's not only well within the image on the screen, now diffused to households across the island by community t-v at the dinner hour, she's butting me with her bowsprit at the rib and on my shoulder (like impatiently), like a spoiled pet demanding attention! Now and then, while speaking on camera in response to the interviewer's question, I turn away slightly, and shove the Ruler back out to sea.

In our supermarket, the other day, the male cashier would say to me: "I saw that video where you were talking about growing up on the islands. I especially liked what I saw of you and your boat. Tethered the way you had her, it was like you and a pet of yours!"

Now, I'd thought, here goes a man who appreciates Culture in all its kaleidoscopic dimensions. And I was tempted to share with him a passage I'd written about me and my boat a year ago, after a boating trip with my grandson, Adrian at the helm. [That story, in fact, is related within this volume.]

In the meantime, there's this dialogue going on between me and the Ruler that the video—and therefore, the folks viewing at home—cannot capture: "Yes! Chuck and poke me in the back, with your unruly self! Make me fall face forward into this bayside water for dramatic effect! You always do as you wish, anyway!"

"Just what are you preening about, Mr. Cultural expert? All you've done with your life is hardly any different from what I've done with the Sea under me!"

"Yeah! We've basically flowed with the Tide! You got it right! We're even! As long as you remember, Bronze Ruler or no Bronze Ruler, your duty to bring me back to port, no matter where I—like our

Dad, the original Freebird— might slinger on the Sea!"

SO WE'VE LIVED

Landmarks, House plots and a Fishing spot

Plunger has lived on several Caribbean islands between the latitudes twelve and twenty. During these sojourns he has engaged scores of islanders of various ages and stations in life in recollections about the life they've lived and the changes they've witnessed. He has also poked around in Church records and other registers and has been approached often enough with some faded and tattered document by people seeking a clarification or translation to sustain or support a claim. In what follows, he attempts to knit together a quilt of pertinent experiences and reflections of these folk. Fact, fiction and family lore mingle. So, here goes:

Rather than preparing his breakfast, as he usually does, this morning Plunger has made his way almost to the end of his block to the MoJo Café with its outdoor umbrella'd tables. While waiting for his order of coffee and a "sandwich meal" of egg, ham, biscuit and home fries, he finds himself slipping into and snapping out of a melancholic apnea driven, he believes, by a certain repugnance towards his immediate surroundings, a disposition, he thinks, which is driving more and more his writings these days, one that, he is concerned, might reserve for him the place of misanthrope and killjoy in the sparse annals of his island's Cultural History.

[From the Marriage records of one of these island churches: Genevieve Eulalie was born on October 17, 1890 at Mingo Bay, the daughter of Mathilde Severin and Alfonso Severin. She is listed as Lutheran. The same record (for the year 1912) informs us that Genevieve married Agustin Belsol, who was born in St. Thomas on March 5, 1885 and who was 27 years old and a Lutheran. He was the son of Manuel Belsol and Angele "Gigi" Belsol. Concerning the first Severin's and the first Belsols on this island, it is recorded in a document having to do with the construction of that first solid stone and mortar two storey that one used to see, on entering the island's main harbor, to the right of the dock, that the builder was Jean Bernard Severin, reportedly born in Hispaniola and living on St. Thomas, and his assistant was a man who bore the last name Belsol, who had come here from Africa.]

[Jean Bernard was the father of Algeron who was

the father of Genevieve. A brother of Algeron was Rufus. Agustin Belsol would appear to have been the grand-son of that first Belsol out of Africa and the son of Manuel and Angele Belsol. Might the two tradesmen, over a warm lunch or a cool drink, have engaged in speculative matchmaking leading many years later to the union of Austin and Genevieve? A cursory glance at our genealogical records tells us that more often than not there was good reasoning to the rhyme behind many of these unions.

[The 1913 record informs us that James Paulus was born on St. John on the 15 of July, 1887; he was 25 years old and a Moravian. He married Consuelo Wentie Severin, who was born on St. John on March 11, 1885 and was 27 years old, a Lutheran and the daughter of Rufus Severin and Marion Francis.]

According to a close cousin of Plunger's, "Gigi" Belsol, in the course of a dispute with James Paulus over property or livestock, dropped to her knees and cursed him and his generations to follow.

And now, in his reverie over the MoJo breakfast sandwich meal, it was Plunger's great aunt's turn to speak, the aunt of his father. And his turn to listen!

What a full-bodied voice and presence she projected despite her simple and frugal life and bearing! Dine was a pillar of the Lutheran church of the town. On any Sunday that they came across the Sound to the island, at the very entry to the bay they could hear her robust countryside bass voice harmonizing hymns beneath and at once over the voices of the choir and congregation.

"Don' take me fo' no Gigi Belsol; I never put a cuss on a mortal!" he could clearly imagine her declaring, as she referenced the fatal—and still active—spell reportedly cast on a cousin of hers and on his issue by her murdered husband's mother. Plunger could hear that stout voice of hers bellowing forth the clarification. For, the record needed to be set straight, since the two women bore French first names and derived nicknames that could get confused: Genevieve, somehow rendered "Dina" or "Dine," and Angele reduced to "Gigi," in the case of her husband's mother—her titular comadre (for good or for bad, but especially in times of need).

No one in Dine's lineage had been known to dabble in spells or curses against other persons, and it wasn't going to start now, especially through possible confusion of nicknames— and a "cyat an' bull" story over a goat!

Dine had her own cross to bear, and bear it she did with fitting dignity and a stiff upper lip. Her young husband, a fisherman, had had this dispute over who knows what and had been killed right there on the bay, next to his boat. Left to fend for herself and the three boys she'd borne him, she promptly disabused potential suitors of their fantasies by declaring that she was "no Dina free c—t!"
For, her choice of words was as salty and to the point as it gets!

Plunger recalls her asking him about his family. When he mentioned the three girls they had, she promptly prescribed corrective measures: "You have to take out yo' gun and shoot in de corna!"

And her acts of charity and custody towards the children of the extended family had a broad reach, even when nudged by the long arm of the Law. Plunger's younger brother remembers the day, when pursued closely by the island's police sergeant for siphoning fuel from a Public Works truck, he and a friend dashed to her house. To the sergeant's query, since he'd distinctly seen them run that way, Dine replied:

"My dear Sir, I don't know when last I've seen any of dose boys!"

In this port village of Cruz Bay, two minutes from the public docks, if you've just landed and proceeded straight ahead from the dock, less than a hundred feet, then turned to the right, then continued on to the first intersection, precisely at the intersection in question, you'll see, facing each other diagonally on your right and on your left, two very simple wooden houses, dwellings from another era. The little house Plunger lives in is one of these two—the one inside the angle—, and it sits on a sixty by ninety foot lot, bordered, as is implied above, on two sides by the public thoroughfare.

The lone impediment, apart from the public thoroughfare, to direct communication between these two early 20th century remnant dwellings is an artless octagonal sign nailed to a four-foot high picket that reads crudely "Slow Down; Iguana Crossing."

"These fetching upstart newcomers," Plunger thinks, as he sips on his coffee. "Smack on the front lawn of my father's aunt's property! May her soul find Peace!"

Now, retreat back to the terrace snackbar by the first intersection you passed, upon leaving the dock, (Yes, the Mojo Café!) and you'll see, on the façade of the jewelry store that occupies a spot in the remnant of the ruins abutting his father's uncle's modest wooden house of the same period (of which all that is left is a replica which is painted on the inside wall of Mooie's Bar, across the street,) the sign "The Purple Turtle." May that great-uncle's soul also find respite and solace from the vulgar and rampant Real Estatism that has swooped down on this rock in the Caribbean! As for the solid mason two storey building mentioned earlier—built by the man whose real name was John Bernadine, the first Sprauve documented on the island, that was gobbled up by the north wing of the "Bayside Mall."

Much of the land between the Iguana and the Turtle, in earlier years, comprised a mixed plot of wetlands and guinea grass pastureland. The wetlands aspect made it an ideal habitat for our land crab. (As such, when a horse, mule or donkey fed and restored here overnight, before returning to the yoke or saddle for country work the following day, one made sure to stake it out around the edges, to guard against the fractured leg in a crab hole.)

Now, this simple one-family dwelling that sits on the flank of the hill was where Tan Dine, granddaughter of John Benardine, spent her last days before passing on. She had lived to a ripe old age, having been widowed when her three sons were boys barely apprenticed in the maritime trade to their lone maternal uncle, himself the youngest brother and one living survivor of the sea-accident most famously associated with the history of the island.

"That day the whole island of St. John fell into deep mourning, and that was the way it was for months afterward," is the way old-timers recalled the event. The news that caused the sorrow and strife? The sailboat returning the cricket team from its match on St. Thomas, had capsized south of that island under the assault of a sudden squall! Two of the Dine's brothers had perished!

Tan Dine, one of the two longest surviving of several sisters of the two brothers—among others—lost at sea in that accident, in those times, lived further uphill, beyond the house on the corner of the Iguana, on this hillside that helped to make of Cruz Bay the haven it was for sea transport between, St. John and British Virgin Islands ports of Jost van Dyk, Tortola and further east and an entrepôt for eastern St. Thomas.

Up there, at mid slope, where she and her youngest son lived in the yet earlier days, (the other two having gone off to War, after training in Sea trade with the Deep Sea Company that fished for sharks north of the islands) one had a good view of sea traffic in the Sound, especially the sailboats leaving the port and those on the final two tacks on the returning trips from the west. In fact, making one's way up the hill to her house, for the young great-nieces and nephews, had its likeness to the Skipper's science of navigating the constant southeast wind that tracks across the sound the better part of the year. For, you climbed that hill in zigzag fashion, replicating the tacks and jibes of the sailboats on their return course to port. So, as kids, Plunger now recalls, they traipsed up that path, in zigzag fashion, (learning in this way something about other distances between two points!) on their visit to their dad's aunt, this stocky, gray-haired lady with the piercing eyes, welcoming smile and empathy-filled voice. "So alyo' race each odda up de hill to fine Tan Dine? As if yo' t'ink I was goin' out, an' alyo' go miss me!"

"But yo' coulda been gone fishin', Tan Dine!"

"Fishin' is fo' later in de aftanoon, w'en de sun goin' down! It too hot, dis time o' de day!"
"We could go fishin' 'round de rocks wid yo', Tan Dine?"

"An' w'e part de soja crab dat I need fo' bait, dat alyo' promise me? Don' bodda tell me! I know! De big one-dem gettin' buckish an' already followin' gyurl frocktail, an' ain' got no time fo' Dine…,an' de li'l one-dem 'fraid o' crab claw! Who de cyap fits, wear it! Whatever alyo' do, jus' remember Dine tell yo' to keep yo' head on!"

"But, Tan Dine, we see yo' wid yo' old paint pan o' fry bait an' yo' bamboo pole, headin' to Firs' Rock de odda day. An' since it had fry in de bay we leave de sojas live anodda day! Like you yo'self duz tell us: Waste not, want not!"

"Pshaaw! Da was las' week! Fry duz come and fry duz go wid de moon! Anyway, good t'ing I had save t'ree-four soja from last trip. W'en de sun go down…,but I don' wan' no tail followin' me today! It got a good size oldwife tiefin' me bait fo' de laas week now, an' I need to concentrate good fo' he; I don' need a bunch o' talk-talk children addlin' meh brain! As fo' de sweets w'a alyo' come here lookin' fa in de firs' place, alyo' come too late! De same one-dem w'a alyo' pass goin' down de road, w'en yo' was comin' up, dey get de laas o' de sugar cake w'at I had."

Even as she would ward them off and dampen their unspoken gluttony for her delectable goodies with unasked for intelligence about the competition, she would be already actively scratching around her little living room, reaching above a ledge here, opening a "safe" there, feeling into a sack hanging behind a door, to access some small treasure to eventually deal out to them.

And, from one of them in the group, intent on mending the broken pact with Tan Dine on soja bait for her fishing: "Tan Dine, we know where it got soja knockin' daag! Soja cyaan' done!"

"Oh yeah? Tell me 'bout it!"

"Shhsh! Don' say it out loud!" another one warns.

Oops, too late! "But 'tis a funky pla...!"

"Funk...WHAT, chile? Where yo' fine dat word? Dine don' want to hear dat word outta alyo' mout', yo' hear? Das a big people word!"

"Well..., 'tis a place dat got all kind 'o rank smell, like congo root an' rottin' fruit, and dey say, a funny wite man who had own de place..."

"Shhsh! Yo' cayaan be duz hear good! She say, she don' wan' none o' dat kind o' talk!"
"So, now yo' talkin' 'bout Estate Adrian, da lan' behind God back w'a used to belong to de buckra from SanaCruz long time back an' w'a meh nephew gone an' buy? Alyo' really listenin' to big people evil talk! Listen to me good: When people don' see, den

dey say! An' it got dem who say 'tis de spirit o' crazy Boman who had own de estate befo' ting get bad, an' it had to sell out. An' it got dose who say 'tis de spirit o' we own nega people w'a de buckra mistreat den fire an' t'row off de lan'!, callin' dem lazy good-fo'-nottin! Tan Dine don' bring dem nor carry dem, wid de evil talk! An' Tan Dine say to alyo', leave it where yo' find it!"

Firs' Rock

Who could dispute Tan Dine on funky haunts and evil tongues? Though she lived on side of this hill that was swept continually by a gentle easterly breeze, her prime fishing spot you reached by a ten-minute walk, beginning with the descent to the town's main street at its western spur, then one trekked 'long de bay,' flanking the part of the port that flushed only during storms, next, cutting through the island's main cemetery, a place called "Found-out" by the elders, before traversing the public dump which was set afire every late afternoon. With favorable winds, the smoke and fume went the other way.

The fishing task is about to start. First, the "mash" is prepared. To do this, a few sojas must be pulled from their shells and have their juicy tails separated from their main body which consists mainly of claws and hairy legs. Dine has mastered the art of coaxing the soja out of the shell; that is, his main body, since the tail is firmly wrapped around the innermost coil of the shell at this point. The trick is to set him face down, so he attempts to crawl. She snaps him up, flicks him over and grabs the exposed body, being careful not to offer him the flesh of a finger! For, when that happens, there is no enticement that will convince the soja to loosen his bite!

So, (with no kids around today) Tan Dine will not be distracted as she extricates the hermit crab from the whelk shell he's chosen for a moveable residence. She's muttering words of self-caution: "Yes, you! Yo' t'ink I don' see yo' two tricky eye-dem squintin' from inside yo' shell at me! Yo' look like a special bad egg w'a plan to put a big claw on Dine l'il finga today! But Dine got news fo' you! Out! Out!" as she clamps down and pulls the little monster, tail and all, clear of its shell! (Dine was like that with all God's little creatures which she called "sinners." In this way she warned: "Shoo fly, don' bother me!" two or three times before swatting at a buzzing nuisance.)

Having separated the bulbous and juicy soja tail from the body, she skillfully loads up her hook with the former and places the main body consisting of carapace with legs and claws, on a flat rock. She pulverizes the crab's body, along with its shell and tosses into the seawater this handful of chum, which we call "mash." Immediately she perceives the flash of light blue that tells her the old wife is among the early feeders.

"Good yo'!" Dine mutters. "Mr. Old Wife, today you go meet yo' match! But firs' , take all de time yo' need to enjoy yo' laas suppa!"

A man called Chick-Feed and Lady Armstrong's filly mule colt.

When our ole man hired Mr. F as caretaker of Estate Adrian, he had by now come to accept that the farming project held little or no promise of even a break-even return. The new personnel, who could, from time to time, recommend in turn the hiring of a day laborer or two for cleaning the pastures, was the result of an act of what today is called "downsizing."

It's not that the land at Adrian was hopelessly poor. To the contrary, people sang its praises as some of the most fertile ground on the island, and many a local bragged about seeing that "rich, dark" soil yield jumbo sweet potatoes and giant tomatoes. (It's as if, where soil was concerned, in our people's mind, the darker, the richer! Never mind the frequent droughts and pummeling from the tropic sun rays that dried and parched the produce on the vine or branch!)

But even more serious an obstacle for the truck-farming side of the Adrian project was a bundle of issues having to do with property and "belonger" status. (Persons who understand the origin of the word "Sooner" in the vocabulary of Americans will have a fuller grasp of the issues I mention here.) For, the ole man, though born on the island, had shipped out as a youth to the neighboring one where he had become something of a modest somebody, a status that made possible the acquisition of the farm.

However, the owner of the adjacent one—no less a local "somebody"— had stayed put and had, in fact, acquired his holding, following related bankruptcies among the landed gentry, sooner! Fencing was of little effect in discouraging the livestock invasions from the adjacent property.

Now, Mr. F worked the estate under the supervision of a certain Mr. B, also paid by the ole man, a man who completely embodied authority and order on the island of a level only attained by bombas during Slavery times. One would expect that Mr. F's supervisor would take on the owner of the trespassing livestock.

However, this Mr. B was a close friend of the

adjacent owner, a riding partner and companion on wild hog raids. So what was the solitary Mr. F, a man well into his sixties, at least at the time, and also a stranger from the larger island with—worse still—suspected roots in the neighboring British one to the north, to do but keep re-planting and repairing fences! By day, anyway!

For, Mr. F was said to be a lay preacher, which raised suspicions on an island that was still at that time only solidly Moravian and Lutheran! And he reputedly traveled to the eastern end of the island several nights every month to preach the word. It would surprise no one to learn that his detractors had it that his late night activities away from the farm in the woods had to do with prowling for female companionship! Could this be why they nicknamed him "Duster" and "Chickfeed?" Both names seem to suggest enticements he might be accused of employing. Who knows?

But, about this time, with the cattle sold off, along with the goats and sheep and the two mules, assuredly, on the counsel of Mr. B, a breeding experiment took place at Adrian. Lady Armstrong, the racing horse the ole man had purchased on the larger island, considered one of a kind on the island in pedigree, was brought to stud with a horse jack on loan from the Agriculture Station in the BVI. ("Horse jack" is the word used by locals to designate a male ass, taller than the average, used to mate with a mare horse.)

The fruit of this coupling was a female mule that would grow to be larger than any of her kind on the island. And no less indomitable! With no cattle on the land, Armstrong's mule colt, as she came to be called, had endless acres on which to graze and cavort. And that is all she did.

So, now, Mr. F had a worldly and worthwhile mission staring him down. One that promised to validate him in the eyes of a suspicious and cynical island community! And, despite his age, he had come to the island with a reputation as a competent horseman!

He would break Armstrong's mule colt! No one had succeeded in doing so yet. Mr. F had a plan; it involved loading gunny sacks—what we call "cruda bags"—on the mule, tying her under a tree for many hours, so she would get a notion of who was boss, then mounting her.

This writer was not present during any of this activity. He can only speculate that the catching and loading of the mule colt involved considerable assistance, men on the ground, so to speak. As for the mounting of the beast, he is told that the old man made his descent from a branch above where she was tethered to the trunk of one of the farm's famous mango trees, supposedly well tired out from the hours of bearing the load mentioned.

It is reported that Mr. F managed to land on the mule colt's back, but lasted there a mere fraction of a second, being summarily tossed to the ground right away, and enjoying enough good fortune to not be trampled by the mule.

These events took place in the waning days of Estate Adrian as a farm. Mr. F passed on a few years later. As for Lady Armstrong's mule colt, she simply would not be ridden. She continued to roam the pasture. Then the word got out to Tortola in the British Virgin Islands that there lived on our island this magnificent mare mule that needed only to be broken and put to work. A buyer entered into negotiations with the ole man, and a boat was sent to transport the animal to that island. She managed to be loaded onto the vessel.

Very sadly, when the boat arrived back home, the crew discovered their animal cargo was dead. She had knocked herself around in the hold of the vessel to the point of smashing her brain.

Gilbert A. Sprauve's first literary work, "The Queue," appeared in 1964 in the winter edition of The Literary Review. After a sabbatical from the craft of half a century, during which he taught modern languages in Africa, in the US and at home, he returned to creative writing with *Soundings over Cultural Shoals* (2007), which he translated respectively into *Vagabondages* (French) and *Andanzas* (Spanish). Pell Mell, . . .So We Live! picks up where Soundings left off; more "Variations of Life" in and about the Virgin Islands, from the heart, mind and soul of Virgin Islanders.